"Reading this book is like sitting down with Amish friends over coffee and listening as they answer every question you ever had about their lives and ways and beliefs. This book makes for compelling reading and is an excellent resource for anyone interested in learning more about the Amish."

—MINDY STARNS CLARK, author of *Plain Answers about the Amish Life* and other books

"Brad Igou's *Amish Voices* is a heartwarming compilation of beautiful Amish letters that will move readers to tears and laugh aloud. The stories will stay with readers long after they finish the book and will offer a greater understanding of the Amish faith and lifestyle. Once readers open this book, they won't put it down until they've reached the last page."

—AMY CLIPSTON, bestselling author of *A Welcome at Our Door* and other books

"Covering topics as diverse as Amish origins, dress, ministers' meetings, ordinations, and beards, *Amish Voices* is an insider's look at Amish life. Brad Igou lets the Amish speak, and the stories they tell are wonderful!"

—KAREN JOHNSON-WEINER, author of *Train Up a Child* and coauthor of *The Amish*

"In *Amish Voices*, we get a taste of the reading material found in Old Order homes across North America. We find the words and sentiments of ordinary Amish people, homespun proverbs, and practical wisdom."

—STEVEN M. NOLT, author of *The Amish: A Concise Introduction*

"This book lets the Amish speak in their own voice. Anyone who reads these forthright, plainspoken, and honest reflections will need to give up the notion that the Amish are a people frozen in time."

—**JOHN D. ROTH**, editor of *Mennonite Quarterly Review*

"Hear from the Amish in their own words in this wide-ranging collection of writings spanning decades. An essential compilation of Amish perspectives on the things that matter."

—**ERIK WESNER**, author of *Success Made Simple* and founder of AmishAmerica.com

AMISH
VOICES

A Collection of Amish Writings

BRAD IGOU, *compiler*

HERALD
P R E S S

Harrisonburg, Virginia

Herald Press
PO Box 866, Harrisonburg, Virginia 22803
www.HeraldPress.com

Library of Congress Cataloging-in-Publication Data
Names: Igou, Brad, 1951- compiler.
Title: Amish voices : a collection of Amish writings / Brad Igou, compiler.
Other titles: Amish in their own words.
Description: Harrisonburg : Herald Press, 2019. | "Amish Voices is the
    abridged edition of The Amish in Their Own Words: Amish Writings from
    25 Years of Family Life Magazine, published by Herald Press in 1999."
Identifiers: LCCN 2019000150| ISBN 9781513805832 (pbk. : alk. paper) |
    ISBN 9781513805849 (hardcover : alk. paper)
Subjects: LCSH: Amish--Social life and customs. | Mennonite Church.
Classification: LCC BX8129.A5 A432 2019 | DDC 289.7/3--dc23 LC
record available at https://lccn.loc.gov/2019000150

Unless otherwise noted, Scripture is adapted from the *King James Version
of the Holy Bible* or Luther's *Bibel*. Some is from the *Good News Bible*—Old
Testament: copyright © American Bible Society 1976; New Testament:
copyright © American Bible Society 1966, 1971, 1976.

Amish Voices is the abridged edition of *The Amish in Their Own Words: Amish
Writings from 25 Years of* Family Life *Magazine*, published by Herald Press
in 1999. These excerpts from *Family Life* magazine, Pathway Publishers,
10380 Carter Road, Aylmer, ON N5H 2R3, Canada, are gratefully used
and adapted by permission.

AMISH VOICES
© 2019 by Herald Press, Harrisonburg, Virginia 22803. 800-245-7894.
    All rights reserved.
Library of Congress Control Number: 2019000150
International Standard Book Number: 978-1-5138-0583-2 (paperback);
978-1-5138-0584-9 (hardcover); 978-1-5138-0585-6 (ebook)
Printed in United States of America
Cover and interior design by Merrill Miller
Cover photo by Bill Coleman. © NoToCo, LLC / AmishPhoto.com
Editorial consulting by Rachel Miller

23 22 21 20 19   10 9 8 7 6 5 4 3 2 1

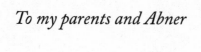
To my parents and Abner

CONTENTS

Preface

"I JUST SAW MY FIRST HORSE AND BUGGY!" So exclaimed a visitor from Australia while walking along the street in the village of Intercourse, Lancaster County, Pennsylvania.

The Amish may sometimes wonder what causes that special fascination that visitors seem to have for them. At first, it is the physical and tangible indicators of their faith—the horse and carriage, the plain way of dress, farming with horses, and so on. Some visitors still think the Amish are really locals paid to dress up and live this way to attract tourists.

The Amish are real, of course, and visitors are naturally fascinated that any group of people living in America would choose to live so differently, without the cars, the Internet, televisions, and other trappings of our technologically advanced society. Amish children walking home from the one-room school, or farmers plowing the fields with horses—these scenes seem to come from another time and place. On a misty morning, the landscape takes on a dreamy, otherworldly atmosphere.

After the excitement of "seeing my first buggy," sensitive visitors start to ponder exactly *who* the Amish are and *why* they live as they do. Some are surprised to discover that "Amish" is the name of a religion, and that they are Christians and not members of some commune or cult. Others want to visit an Amish farm, walk through an Amish home, or stop and talk to the people themselves. Few ever have the chance to do so. With more than eight million visitors coming every year and about forty thousand Amish in Lancaster County, each Amish person would need to "entertain" about two hundred guests a year!

For others, the Amish are a curiosity, making intriguing photography subjects. Few of us would care to be photographed and stared at while going about our daily lives. But the Amish do live in a fishbowl. They do not seek the attention of the world around them. Yet the world seems endlessly fascinated and drawn to their way of life.

How many of us would stand up to such scrutiny? We seem quick to stereotype all Amish people on the basis of the actions of a few. The Amish are the first to admit that they are far from perfect, and suffer from many of the evils of the world around them. Yet most of the Amish understand the curiosity that visitors have for their way of life.

Many books have been written about the Amish, including countless Amish novels, and no year goes by without hundreds of new ones being published. The Amish are also the subject of reality television shows such as *Amish Mafia* and *Breaking Amish*.

With the exception of some high-quality documentaries and books, these portrayals of the Amish tend to range from fairly accurate to ridiculous, offensive, or sensational. The media have spread many false ideas about the Amish. They suffer from being portrayed as ignorant country bumpkins or as saintly people living in utopia. They are, of course, neither.

The task, then, is to see the Amish as they are: as real people, as our friends and neighbors. As in other religious denominations, there are good and "not so good" Amish. Like the rest of us, they sometimes make mistakes, fail to live up to their faith, suffer criticism and ridicule, worry about how to raise their children, and have doubts about themselves. Yet for anyone who has spent a few hours sitting and talking with the Amish, there is also something special about the experience.

After observing and talking to many visitors, I wondered if there were a way to give people a better idea of what the Amish are like as people. I wanted readers to see them not as a monolithic group, but as individuals, families, and communities living in various settlements in the United States and Canada.

Years ago when I was in college, I lived on an Amish farm for three months. There I began to read some publications from a place called Pathway Publishers in Ontario, Canada. This Amish publishing house produces several monthly magazines and many books. The Amish do the writing and manage the company, something unusual. These publications solicit articles and letters from Old Order Amish and Old Order Mennonites all over the United States and Canada.

The Pathway periodicals are unlike *The Budget* (Sugarcreek, Ohio) or *Die Botschaft* (Lancaster, Pa.), newspapers that mainly give short news reports from local communities. Instead, Pathway has tackled areas such as religious interpretation, social issues, and problems of readers. There are articles on church history, church controversies, and even personal problems. Through these three magazines, I discovered a way to "meet" hundreds of Amish and hear their thoughts. The *Blackboard Bulletin* centers on schools and advice for teachers and parents. The *Young Companion* is for young people and offers stories and advice relevant to them as they move toward deciding to join the Amish faith.

Family Life, however, is the magazine that appealed to me the most. In its pages I came to see the Amish as they are, trying to deal with daily problems, applying their faith in a difficult modern world, and sometimes disagreeing with each other on how to do it. I relished the humor revealed in some of the articles, and other times the touching stories moved me to tears.

From this, an idea hatched. I decided to read through the first twenty-five years of this monthly magazine, select a broad range of articles, pull them together in an organized fashion, and make a book. Thus, rather than some outsider writing *about* the Amish, the Amish at last speak *for themselves*. You, the reader, can hear these Amish voices, not from hundreds of years ago, but from recent times, as we moved with them into the twenty-first century. *Amish Voices* is the condensed edition of *The Amish in Their Own Words*, which was published in 1999.

So here is a book about the Amish, written by the Amish. Although I have selected the material, I have tried to keep myself out of it as much as possible so that the writers may emerge with their own character, as neither "odd" nor "saintly."

To include more selections, I have edited many longer articles and condensed some stories, always trying not to destroy the style and message of the writer. The Pathway editorial staff has had an opportunity to check the results and make sure meanings are not altered. And sometimes, articles were so compelling, informative, or well written that I included them whole.

In the following pages, sensitive readers will learn many details of Amish life and religious customs. They also will hear the very human and deep thoughts these people have in their daily lives. Many excerpts are anonymously written or signed only with initials. Most Amish are not likely to engage in intense self-analysis or bare their souls to others. As they wrote their feelings, many, I believe, found a wonderful outlet for their personal concerns. Some people think the Amish are rather stoic; these writings, however, are filled with emotion, joy, and sorrow.

I have grouped the hundreds of selections into chapters by topics. They are not in chronological order, but arranged by subject matter to flow logically from one to another. My own brief introductory remarks, in distinctive type, precede each chapter and some selections. When words of explanation or summary are needed within the quoted articles, they appear in square brackets [like this].

Titles have been copied or supplied from ideas in the articles. A pen name, like a signature, sometimes appears at the end of a piece (for example, "A Girl with an Aching Heart"). Some pieces include the author's name if known (first initial and last name for writers-editors: David Wagler, Joseph Stoll, David Luthy, and Elmo Stoll). Pieces written by the editors or staff are attributed to staff. Those without any attribution are written by contributors wishing to remain anonymous.

Almost all the writers are Old Order Amish, who sometimes use the term *English* to refer to the non-Amish. A few of the shorter pieces are by Old Order Mennonites. Nevertheless, their writings would not be in *Family Life* if they were not in keeping with Amish values.

I thank all these known and unknown contributors whose writings I chose to be part of this project. I trust their words may be educational and inspirational.

Family Life continues to be published. You may wish to subscribe for your own family and friends. To subscribe to *Family Life*, write to Pathway Publishers, 10380 Carter Road, Aylmer, ON N5H 2R3, Canada.

In these pages you will understand, think, laugh, cry, and be touched in a personal way by these individuals, a people at once ordinary and extraordinary, a people focused not so much on this world but on the next. I hope that you, too, will come to call them friends.

—*Brad Igou*
Lancaster, Pennsylvania

ONE

What Is *Family Life?*

FAMILY LIFE STARTED IN 1968 as a monthly magazine "dedicated to the promotion of Christian living among the Plain people, with special emphasis on the appreciation of our heritage." At that time, the staff of writers-editors consisted of David Wagler, assisted by Joseph Stoll, David Luthy, Elmo Stoll, and Sarah Weaver. They estimated they would need 4,000 subscribers for a forty-page magazine, or 5,000 for fifty pages. The subscription price then was four dollars a year.

The April 1969 issue was mailed to 8,149 homes, and to 113 bookstores for resale, in 38 states, 4 Canadian provinces, and 9 foreign countries, including Germany, Australia, and Japan. The states of Pennsylvania, Ohio, and Indiana received the most.

By March 1982, *Family Life* was being sent to over 13,000 homes in 45 states, 8 Canadian provinces, and 13 foreign countries, including India as well as countries in Central and South America. In 1992, paid circulation was 19,000, and by 1998 more than 23,000. In 2010, *Family Life* was being mailed to more than 31,000 subscribers.

In January 1968, the editors at Pathway Publishing in Aylmer, Ontario, began the first issue of their new magazine with the following question:

What Is Family Life*?*

Family Life is the name of the magazine you are holding in your hands. But it is much more. The family is the heart of the community and the church. Even a nation is made up of families. If there is a strong family life, then the church, the community, and the nation will be likewise. If family life degenerates, then all will suffer.

Family life must be translated into terms of everyday living. What can we do to the community? Do we realize that our everyday work should be a God-given opportunity to serve him? Can we appreciate and make the most of the everyday blessings we receive? Do we stop to enjoy God's creation all around us, and the works of his fingers?

This is the goal of *Family Life*—to be an instrument through which thoughts and ideas can be transmitted.

Do not feel that the *Family Life* writers or editors pretend to be experts in this field. Indeed, we often need the helps and inspirations offered in these pages as much as anyone. We hope that by sharing our cupful of oil, it will be increased even as that of the poor widow of Zarephath (see 1 Kings 17:10-16).

Across the Editor's Desk

There is no way of accurately telling the sources of material contributed for *Family Life*. Regarding material arriving from outside the Pathway office, we estimate that it has come from the following writers: 60 percent from Old Order Amish, 30 percent from Old Order Mennonites, and 10 percent from selected or other sources. The Old Order Mennonites, with about 10 percent of the subscribers, are contributing about 30 percent of the material sent in. We appreciate this but can't help wondering what would happen if our Amish readers would send in as much material per subscriber as do the Old Order Mennonites.

—Staff

* * *

We [the editors] are all Old Order Amish, and most of our contributors are either Amish or from related "horse and buggy" groups of Plain people.

—Staff

* * *

Practically everything that goes into *Family Life* is checked carefully by a minister. If it is a doctrinal article or one that is controversial, we like to have several ministers or bishops look it over. After it is published, it goes into nearly every community of Plain folks in the United States and Canada. Anyone who finds anything misleading has the privilege and the responsibility to inform us of it. We have this confidence in our readers that they will let us know if there is anything that will be a hindrance to anyone. Of course, there is often a difference of opinion on some matters due to the fact that no person has a full understanding of any subject.

First Corinthians 13:9 says that we know only in part, but that the time shall come when our knowledge is perfect, but not in this life.

—Staff

* * *

The stories in *Family Life* are either true stories or true-to-life stories. Sometimes a writer takes incidents from the lives of different people and puts them together in one story. The characters in true-to-life stories often make us say, "That's just like someone I used to know."

—Staff

* * *

We once received a story from a man. It sounded so true to life that we thought it probably was a true happening. How surprised we were when the man added at the end of the story, "As far as I know, none of this story is true." We wondered for a moment how he could have written a story that was so real, so true to life, if he got it all from his imagination. But then we saw that he had added, "Please do not sign my name, or my relatives will think I wrote this story about them." The story may not have been true in details, but was true in the ways that really mattered. In attitudes, problems, failures, and habits portrayed, it was true, *too* true.

I wonder how many of our readers realize how much time and effort goes into each of the historical articles that appear in *Family Life*. The historical editor is constantly working on many different projects at the same time and corresponding with hundreds of people. In this way, bits of information are being discovered and assembled on the various topics until there is enough for a whole article on one subject.

—Staff

* * *

A subscriber once wrote to say that there were too many "pat your own back" articles, letters from readers saying how much they like the magazine. The editors agreed and decided not to print letters saying nice things about the magazine, but only comments on particular articles.

Another time a reader wrote to say that because of all of his farmwork, he didn't have time to read everything in *Family Life*. There simply was too much. The editors answered by saying, "If you are too busy to read it, then you're too busy."

Yet another woman explained that she feared she might be neglecting her Bible reading because of the publication. This prompted the editors to respond, "If reading our papers makes you neglect the Bible, we hope you will cancel your subscription."

TWO

Amish Beginnings

THE STORY OF THE AMISH FAITH begins in Zurich, Switzerland, after Martin Luther's historic Reformation. The emergence in 1525 of the Swiss Brethren, or Anabaptists, forebears of the Mennonites and the Amish, is a history as compelling and inspiring as can be found anywhere. Beliefs in adult baptism and separation of church and state were viewed as a threat both to Huldrych Zwingli's Reformed Church and to the local government, with which it was allied. Thousands of these "radicals" were put to death in the following years.

Accounts of their individual stories are found in books like the *Martyrs Mirror* (in print from 1660) and the *Ausbund* (songs from 1535, in print from 1564), the hymnal used in Amish worship services. These are stories of pacifism and persecution, love and peace amid hatred and violence, a testimony to faith and survival at horrible costs. Upon arriving in America, the Amish faith grew and prospered, with each generation finding new and different challenges forced on them by the times.

Early Anabaptists

Felix Manz was born in 1498 in Zurich, Switzerland. He received a very good education, and when Huldrych Zwingli founded his Reformed Church, Felix joined him. But it was not long before Felix felt that Zwingli had not broken far enough away from the Catholic Church, especially concerning baptism. Because Zwingli continued to baptize babies, Felix and some others broke away and founded a church in which only adults were baptized. He was the first of the Swiss Brethren to give his life for the faith [in a Reformed area. Bolt Eberli was burned at the stake in a Catholic canton, May 29, 1525].

Felix was drowned on January 5, 1527, by order of the Zurich city authorities. He and Conrad Grebel are considered the founders of the Anabaptist movement in Switzerland, and our Amish churches today can count him a forefather in faith.

Georg Blaurock's life could fill a book, as it was very eventful. It should suffice to say that he was a Catholic monk who joined the Anabaptists in the early years of the movement. He was baptized by Conrad Grebel and was a fellow worker with him and Felix Manz. Georg was a forceful and eloquent preacher, and very zealous. Many times he was cast into prison, punished, and banished, yet he remained true to the faith. He died a martyr's death in 1529, being burned at the stake.

—D. Luthy

Children of Martyrs

We Plain people often refer to our ancestors, the Anabaptists. Willingly, they offered up their lives and accepted death. Hardly a sermon is preached in our churches today without some mention being made of our forebears and what they suffered.

Many of our homes have a copy of the *Martyrs Mirror*, well over a thousand pages, telling us about our ancestors in the faith, how they suffered, what they believed, and why they died. Yet we are so busy with our daily work that we seldom find time or interest to read this monumental book.

Take Michael Sattler, for instance. His story is only one of the hundreds in the *Martyrs Mirror*. His sentence has been recorded for us, preserved down through the years: "Judgment is passed that Michael Sattler shall be delivered to the executioner, who shall cut out his tongue, then throw him upon a wagon, and tear his body twice with red-hot tongs; and after he has been brought without the gate, he shall be pinched five times in the same manner."

Notice that they took out his tongue at the outset. The martyrs were famous for letting their tongues be heard during their last moments. They would shout aloud to their fellow believers, or they would entreat their persecutors to think seriously about what they were doing.

So the first thing the judges decreed was that Michael Sattler be relieved of his tongue. Then, bring on the hot tongs.

With these preliminaries taken care of, Michael was sentenced to be burned alive. They tied him to a wooden stake, binding him hand and foot.

However, Michael's testimony was not to be hindered by the loss of his tongue. He had told fellow believers beforehand that if he still remained faithful to God, he would lift two fingers aloft as a sign.

As the flames leapt around him, as the heat scorched his body and the pain seared him mercilessly, Michael must have struggled with almost superhuman strength to retain consciousness. At last the ropes that bound his wrists were severed. Mustering his faltering strength, he lifted his arm aloft, two fingers outstretched toward heaven. There can be no doubt: the final act of Michael Sattler inspired and breathed courage and renewed boldness into more onlookers than any mere words his tongue could have uttered.

We are children of martyrs! That phrase sets us apart from other people. There's only one problem. If we do not have the spirit of the martyrs, but shrink from hardships, from self-denial, from sacrifice, from a life of discipline and restraint— then the martyrs were not our forebears at all, and we are not their children.

If we have the spirit of this world, loving ease and pleasure and luxury and leisure, we are the children of the prince of this world [John 12:31]. We are only deceiving ourselves if we then talk of the martyrs as being our ancestors. The simple truth is, unless we follow in their footsteps, we are not their children.

—E. Stoll

The Decisions We Make

In 1632, the Dutch Mennonites gathered at Dordrecht [Dordt, or Dort] in Holland and reached agreement on eighteen basic articles of doctrine, which we know as the Dordrecht Confession of Faith. These Mennonites, we believe, still held and practiced the doctrines of the earlier Anabaptists of the preceding century, when Menno Simons and Dirk Philips were living. These were Dutch Mennonites and not the group of [Swiss Brethren Anabaptist] churches that later came to be known as Amish.

At the time the Dordrecht Confession was drawn up, many of the Dutch Mennonites were already becoming wealthy and adapting themselves to the ways and wisdom of the world. During the next sixty years, the Dutch Mennonites rapidly changed their thought and practices. In the end, it was the churches of Alsace and southern Germany who were best able to retain the original faith of the Anabaptists as summarized in the eighteen articles of the Dordrecht Confession. [These churches in Alsace and southern Germany were composed largely of Swiss Brethren Anabaptists who had fled persecution in Switzerland. Their ministers, led by bishop Jacob Ammann, were firm supporters of the Dordrecht Confession.]

Although a church division resulted, Ammann was successful in getting most of the churches in that region to join him in a move toward greater discipline and strictness, and in a closer adherence to the Dordrecht Confession.

We can sum up the beliefs and concerns of the Amish group as follows:

1. Adherence to the eighteen articles of the Dordrecht Confession of 1632.

2. Additional standards and restrictions were needed in dress and modes of living, to keep worldly trends out of the church.

3. Resistance to change, not only in church administration, but also in everyday living. It is essential that the church be resistant to change, and consent to it only when there is a clear and definite need (and then only if it is the right direction).

4. A solid foundation to ensure the continuity of the church without depending upon any certain person or persons. If our bishop or ministers are called away in death tomorrow, we should have the confidence that others will fill the empty places and the church will be able to continue.

—D. Wagler

Two Waves of Amish Migration to America

So far, no historian has been able to pinpoint the exact date the first Amish settler arrived in America. Without a doubt,

Amish immigrants had settled in Pennsylvania before 1737, which year marks the definite coming of the largest group of Amish settlers in that century. What the *Mayflower* is to the Puritans, the ship *Charming Nancy* is to the Amish. When it docked at Philadelphia on October 8, 1737, it had on board some twenty-one Amish immigrants.

Amish pioneers continued to arrive in America every few years until nearly the beginning of the Revolutionary War in 1775. During the last quarter of that century, no Amish are known to have reached America's shores. Many more, however, came during the following century. Since so much time elapsed between the Amish who immigrated in the 1700s and those who came during the 1800s, historians speak of the "first and second waves" of Amish migration.

No accurate count of the Amish immigrants and their families can be made, but historians estimate that fewer than five hundred men, women, and children came during the "first wave" of migration in the 1700s. In sharp contrast to that number are the estimated three thousand who arrived during the 1800s. Most Amish today descend from the "first wave" of immigrants.

It must be pointed out that during each century, descendants of non-Amish immigrants have added their surnames to Amish society. Some entered as orphans and joined the Amish church when they grew to maturity. Others seemingly joined in order to marry, choosing, though, to remain the rest of their lives. And some were converts who joined because of religious convictions.

Of the many such surnames present today among the Amish, only five entered during the 1700s: Headings, Glick, Keim, Renno, and Riehl. On the other hand, thirty-two surnames are among those who entered during the 1800s.

The descendants of the "second wave" immigrants, added to converts, form a more significant portion of Amish society today than historians have previously thought.

Records show that some Amish immigrants from Europe were on the ocean for as little as 54 days to as long as 120 days.

—D. Luthy

The Northkill Amish

Because of its size and early founding, the Lancaster Amish settlement in Pennsylvania was often thought to have been the first Amish settlement in America. But it wasn't. In 1740, an Amish settlement was flourishing in Berks County, Pennsylvania. Known as the Northkill settlement, it was located near the present town of Hamburg, Pennsylvania.

In the 1730s, Northkill began receiving settlers from the Amish settlement in Switzerland. By 1749, the settlement had received its first minister, Jacob Hertzler, who was later ordained bishop through a letter sent from bishops in Switzerland. The French in Canada stirred up the Indians to attack various settlements in Pennsylvania, for they did not like the Germans and English settling there. Because of the raids, the Amish left the Northkill settlement less than twenty years after its establishment. They moved to other parts of Berks County, and sometime later to Lancaster County.

On June 27, 1959, a state historical marker was erected commemorating the Northkill settlement:

NORTHKILL AMISH
The first organized Amish Mennonite congregation in America. Established by 1740. Disbanded following Indian attack, September 29, 1757, in which a Provincial soldier and three members of the Jacob Hochstetler family were killed near this point.

—D. Luthy

One Dark Night

Following is an account, in story form, of a French-led Native American attack on the Hochstetler family [fictionalized in the Return to Northkill series by Ervin Stutzman]. It was reprinted in an issue of *Family Life* as it appears in *Our Heritage*, a book for the eighth grade in the Pathway Reading Series for Amish schools.

The Northkill settlement was established in 1739 close to what is now Harrisburg, Pennsylvania. Indians also lived in the area. While William Penn governed the territory, they were peaceful and friendly. But after his death in 1718, misunderstandings arose, caused at least in part by Thomas Penn's cheating the Indians.

When the French and Indian War broke out in 1754, conditions were ripe in Pennsylvania for conflict between the Indian peoples and the white settlers. The once quiet and peaceable frontier became the scene of violent raids, bloodshed, death, and terror.

All summer at Northkill, there had been reports of raids and unrest. The Amish families did not risk having many gatherings. But as fall came, tension seemed to have lessened, and the Jacob Hochstetler family invited the young people to their home for an apple-schnitzing and an evening of fellowship. It was a pleasant evening.

As the Hochstetlers said goodbye to their friends, little did they know that tragedy and death stalked the woods about them.

Attacked

"Jacob, Jacob. Wake up!"

Jacob Hochstetler groaned sleepily, and then with a start he was wide awake. In the dim light that found its way through the narrow window in the log cabin, he could see his wife bending over him. Jacob could not see the fear in her eyes, but cold shivers went up his back as he caught the alarm in her voice. "Jacob, there's something . . . there's something going on outside."

Instantly, Jacob remembered the reports of Indian raids they had heard all summer. Could anything like that happen to them? "What was it? What did you hear?" he asked in a low voice, swinging his feet out and sitting on the bed.

"The dog barked, barked so suddenly, so strangely, as if something surprised him. There was something about it that I just couldn't help thinking . . ."

"I heard it too, Mom," someone spoke from the adjoining room. It was young Jake, their third son. His voice was calm and reassuring in the quietness of the cabin. "It is probably nothing," he said. "I'll go to the door and look out." The lad jumped from his bunk along the wall.

His father started to speak, started to say, "Wait, let me go," but did not.

Slowly, young Jake unbolted the heavy door and stood there, straining to see in the dim light of the waning moon. The night seemed so quiet, so friendly and peaceful.

Without warning, the night was shattered by a bloodcurdling whoop. A shot rang out. With a sharp cry of pain, the unsuspecting boy half fell, half leaped back into the protecting shelter of the cabin. His father sprang to the door and with trembling fingers slipped the bolt into position.

"Jacob, my son, are you hurt?" gasped the anxious father.

"I don't think it's serious," the brave boy replied. "The shot struck me in the leg."

"Shall I light a lamp?" shuddered Mrs. Hochstetler.

"No, no," answered her husband. "What we do must be done in the dark. They could see us too clearly if we had a light."

The two oldest boys, Joseph and Christian, and their only sister were awakened by the commotion. They joined the group huddled together in the center of the cabin.

"Maybe they have left," Christian ventured after they waited in silence a few minutes. "Let me go to the window and look out." Stealthily he crept to the window and peeped into the darkness. "There they are," he whispered, pointing with his finger. His father and Joseph stood close behind him, following his gaze. "Right there by the outdoor oven. Can you see them?"

A half dozen tall dusky figures moved in the shadowy darkness.

They appeared to be counseling.

"Quickly, now's our chance," Joseph said, grabbing his rifle from the wall and directing Christian to do likewise. "I'll wait until you're ready, and we'll shoot together."

Joseph felt a restraining hand on his shoulder. "No, boys," Mr. Hochstetler said. "It's wrong to kill. We cannot do that."

"But if we don't shoot, they will kill us. Jacob is already wounded."

"No, no," replied the older man firmly. "You know it is not right to harm another, even to protect ourselves."

"But think, Father, we have plenty of powder and shot here. We could hold them off until daylight, and then they will leave."

"No, we will not shoot. We will trust in God, boys." There was a note in Jacob Hochstetler's voice that told his sons further begging was useless; the decision was final.

Was something moving outside? The family could not be certain. They thought they heard a stone click. The dog barked, but he was not at the house. The bark seemed to come from the top of a nearby hill. At one corner of the cabin sounded the grate of something rubbing. Breathlessly, the Hochstetlers waited. All was quiet except for their breathing—loud and rasping with tenseness. A rustling noise, a crackling sound, and the Hochstetlers knew without speaking that the thing they had feared was upon them: the Indians had set fire to their house.

Through the chinks in the wall, they could see the eerie glow of the leaping flames. Smoke stung their nostrils.

After the warm summer, the logs of the cabin were dry, and caught like tinder. The trapped family could feel the warmth of the blaze as they crouched low on the floor to escape the choking fumes of the thickening smoke.

To go out would be suicide. That was exactly what the waiting men expected and were prepared for. There would not be the slightest chance of escape.

"Let's go to the cellar," the younger Jacob suggested. They closed the door tightly behind them to keep the smoke from following. The damp cellar was crowded and even darker than the smoke-filled cabin had been, but at least they could breathe.

Silently they prayed and waited while the fire raged above them. They had fled its punishing heat for a moment, but they knew that like a relentless monster cheated of its prey, it would follow them, and there would be nowhere else to go. With a splintering crash, one section of the roof collapsed, shaking the beams in the cabin floor and sending a shower of fine dust upon them.

Christian choked and then sneezed, but it was only a stifled faint little sound drowned out by the growing roar of the fierce fire raging above their heads.

As the fire burned on, the strangling heat engulfed them in the shallow cellar. At one end the floor above burned through, just a tiny red eye glaring at them in the inky blackness. Then like a glowing cancer, it spread and grew.

Stumbling against a large wooden barrel, Jacob Hochstetler was struck with an idea. With the desperateness of a drowning man, he seized upon it. Fumbling with the tight-fitting cover, he exclaimed, "Why don't we splash this apple juice on the fire? It might slow it down."

Carefully he splashed a dipper of the liquid on the angry hole of fire. It sizzled and spat back like an angry cat, but its rage was noticeably dampened. They did it again and again; for a moment the fire was checked. The family began to hope. Then the dipper scraped the bottom of the barrel, and they knew it was empty.

A wall fell in, and a shower of sparks shot through the flame-eaten boards at a dozen places. Smoke poured down, and the heat was unbearably intense.

"Couldn't we escape through the window?" Joseph asked. "Maybe they have left by now." With strong arms he wrenched the sturdy window frame loose and looked outside. The gray dawn was breaking over the wooded hills of Pennsylvania.

With a glad cry of joy he turned and exclaimed, "It's beginning to be daylight outside, and I see no one around."

"Wait a minute," the father said. "Here is something that may come in use." He held up a small basket of peaches from the cellar floor. "Stuff these in your pockets, boys, in case we have to hide in the woods a few days." Quickly, the boys grabbed a few of the firmer fruits, and then one by one the family squeezed through the narrow opening and gathered in a thankful circle beside the smoldering ruins of their home.

Captives

With the coming of dawn, the wary Indians had melted farther and farther into the comforting protection of the nearby forest. When they saw no sign of life from the cabin, they were at last satisfied that the inhabitants had perished. Silently they turned to follow unmarked trails through the wilderness to their teepee homes.

Then they heard a shout and halted in their tracks. One young Indian boy had lingered behind to eat peaches in the Hochstetler's fine hillside orchard. Thoroughly enjoying his feast on the white man's fruit, he was astonished to see the entire family emerge, alive and well, from the burned building. It took only a shout and a moment to recall his departing companions. For the Hochstetler family, just escaped from the cabin furnace, the shrill call of the Indian lad resounded with tragedy.

Immediately the small group was surrounded. As the Indians closed in, Joseph sprang and broke through, running with incredible fleetness. Two men followed him in close pursuit, but Joseph was an able runner and finally shook them off. Then he lay hiding behind a large log, resting while his breath came in great tearing gasps and his heart throbbed with fear.

The father and two husky sons offered no resistance as the attackers struck dead three of their number—the mother, young Jake, and the only daughter. One stalwart man swung back his deadly tomahawk over Christian, then changed his mind and took him captive along with his father.

Dazed and in shock, the two grief-stricken survivors were marched away. Later they were joined by Joseph. The warriors had stumbled upon his hiding place and, before he could flee, had captured him. The outlook was dark for the unhappy captives. They were constantly guarded, so there was no possibility of escape.

"Why was I saved instead of my wife?" the sorrowing father wondered as they tramped through the wilderness. He remembered how she had told him earlier in the summer that a band of hungry Indians had come to their cabin one day, while he and the boys were absent. They had asked for food, but for some reason his wife had refused to give them any. They had left disappointed, scowling and muttering angrily. Did the incident have any connection with the fatal nightmare only a few hours behind him? Jacob could only wonder as he walked numbly on and on.

After marching weary miles, the tired party reached an Indian village. The first thing in store for the prisoners was the gauntlet. This was a brutal form of torture to which Indians often put their captives. Standing in two long rows and armed with clubs and whips, the Indians forced the unfortunate victims to run between the two lines. This was a hideous experience, and many fell beneath the cruel blows, unable to make it to the end of the gauntlet.

Jacob and his sons watched in horror as the tribesmen dashed about, picking out whips and stout sticks to be used in beating them. "My God," half prayed and half groaned the weary father, "have we not suffered enough?" Limply, his hands dropped to his side. Then he remembered the peaches they had guarded so carefully since their capture.

"The peaches," he whispered hoarsely to his sons. The Indians were already beginning to line up. The entire village could be seen gathering to watch the sport, curious to know how the weak white men would fare. Standing slightly aloof from the rest with his hands folded solemnly across his chest stood the majestic figure of the chief. Joseph held out the two peaches he had left. Jacob looked at them. "Hardly good enough," the father muttered. They were both badly bruised. Joseph had crushed them when he lay behind the log to hide from his pursuers.

Reaching into his pocket, Christian produced three peaches. They were in much better condition. Taking them quickly from his son, Jacob walked toward the forbidding figure of the great chief.

The chief stared with unblinking eyes at the man before him, his dark handsome face expressionless.

"Here, a gift for you." Jacob smiled and held out the peaches. "For the great chief." Jacob smiled again.

The leader's face changed, and his eyes beamed with pleasure; he was immensely pleased. Jabbering excitedly to his followers, he forbade them to go on with the gauntlet. With a sigh of relief, Jacob turned and joined his waiting sons.

A few days later they were aware of some unusual activity in the camp. "I fear they are going to separate us," Jacob told the boys. His soft eyes filled with sudden tears at the painful thought of parting with the only two sons he had left. He sensed that their time to talk was short. "No matter what happens," he admonished them, "be kind to the Indians. Don't try to resist them. They have used us well since we are at the camp. Act as if you were content, but never give up that you may someday escape. Even if you forget everything else, try to remember your name and the Lord's Prayer."

The anxious father had guessed correctly. With a heavy heart, he was led away to another village. The boys were parted, too, but they were frequently allowed to see each other. They were young and soon grew accustomed to Indian ways.

The cold winter passed. One warm thawing morning in early spring, the boys were united after not seeing each other for a while.

"What's up?" Christian asked, looking at his brother standing in front of him, dressed exactly like an Indian.

"I'm not sure," Joseph replied, "but something is." The Indians were glancing at them and talking excitedly. Finally they seemed to have made up their minds. As they approached the boys, the one who could speak English the best said, "You become brother to Indian." The entire group stood around the boys, smiling pleasantly at them. "We like you," the spokesman went on. "We are brothers. But we do not have this." He pointed to Joseph's beard and then to Christian's.

"You do not have this." He rubbed his own smooth skin.

The boys understood what was happening. They were to be adopted into the tribe. Having their beards plucked out one hair at a time was a painful process, and most of the hair on their heads received the same treatment. The only hair the Indians left untouched was a small tuft at the top of their heads.

Having their hair plucked was not the only thing connected with adoption. There were various ceremonies and Indian rites to be endured. Once they were taken to the river and scrubbed with a stiff brush to wash the white blood from their veins.

Escape

Every day Jacob watched for his chance, but it seemed as if it would never come. The lonesome man wondered if he would ever see his two sons again.

His captors were careful never to tell Jacob where he was, and this made escape even more impossible. If he could escape, which way should he travel? The situation was discouraging.

Slowly the days turned into weeks and the weeks into months. One year passed. Another year came and went. Through three long years of weary days, Jacob Hochstetler waited and prayed and watched and hoped.

"What was that old man doing by his tent?" Jacob wondered as he went quietly about his usual work one morning. His job was to provide food for the camp while the rest of the men were on the warpath.

Without drawing attention to his presence, Jacob worked his way closer to the old man. Several husky warriors were grouped around him, and with a short stick he was making marks on the ground.

"A map!" Jacob gasped under his breath. "If I could only get close enough to see, perhaps I might discover something of where we are. With God's help, I'll escape yet," he resolved.

Pretending to be busy working, Jacob edged closer and closer. It was hard to see clearly, but in the loose dust the old man seemed to be sketching mountains and rivers and forest trails. Jacob caught the words "Settler camp here," and he saw where the stick pointed. Finally, he had a hazy idea of what he longed so much to know. He watched for a chance more closely than ever before.

Under cover of darkness, he slipped away one night while most of the men were away fighting. He knew the Indians would try their best to trail him and bring him back. Carefully he destroyed all signs of his passing, so no one could track him. Constantly he feared he would meet some of the warriors returning from battle.

He traveled miles on foot, mostly by night, taking his directions the best he could from the stars. He had to find his food without shooting, for he did not dare risk being betrayed by the sound of his gun. When he crossed creeks, he would wade upstream to break his scent.

His years with the Indians had taught him wood lore, and now he needed all he had.

Coming upon a river, he fashioned a crude raft with his bare hands, tying the logs together with grapevine ropes.

Day after day he sat on the raft, floating down river. Uncertainty and doubt plagued him. "Am I getting closer to friends and loved ones?" he would wonder. Often a worried look would cross his face, and he would talk to himself. "What if the current is only daily taking me farther into the depth of a trackless wilderness?"

Constantly there was the problem of food. Now and then he chanced upon a few bites of something he could eat, but generally he became hungrier and thinner and weaker. At last his tired body became too starved and weakened to get up, and he could only lie helplessly, staring at the unbroken line of trees as he drifted by.

Suddenly Jacob's dim eyes, clouded with fatigue, opened wide in surprise and disbelief. "Are those really buildings?" He tried to raise his head. "Have I reached a fort at last?" he whispered in near delirium. "Or is it only the feverish working of my mind?"

Jacob struggled desperately to get to his feet, to shout or wave. He was persuaded now that it was a fort. "Have I come this far only to drift by unnoticed, and on to my fate?" With his last bit of feeble strength, he fought to rise, but all he could do was hold one thin hand up. Slowly the dying man floated past the fort, a lonely speck on a wide river. He hoped in vain. There was no shout of recognition. He had not been seen.

Just below the fort at a shallow place in the river, a man stood watering his horse. He looked up and saw the frail raft.

"Whoa," the man exclaimed in surprise. "What do I see?" He stood squinting his eyes, gazing curiously at the drifting object.

"Sure looks like a raft," he observed idly. "But it can't be. I see nothing moving. Probably just an odd-shaped log."

Just then Jacob's arm grew tired. Exhausted with the effort, his hand dropped to his side.

The watching man caught the slight movement. "The thing is alive," he declared to his horse. "It looks like a man too." Mounting his horse, he galloped to the fort to report what he had just witnessed.

Jacob was rescued and given food and kind care. That night in the soft bed at the fort, Jacob closed his eyes and slept the slumber of a grateful man. While others stood in awe and marveled at the hardships he had endured, the worn man quietly rested, secure in the knowledge that his faith in God had brought him back.

Sometime later, a cool summer breeze was blowing as Jacob sat in his cabin, eating his noon meal. He glanced up, slightly startled as a shadow darkened the open doorway.

A tall Indian stood there, silent and straight. He didn't say a word. His glance went all around the cabin, resting briefly on Jacob. Then, turning, he made his way to a stump in the small clearing and sat down. All the while Jacob was eating, he sat there, patiently waiting. "I wonder what he wants?" Jacob mused, finishing his meal and rising from the table. "I guess I had better go out and see."

The tall Indian arose as Jacob approached him. He stood there, eyeing the man before him for a long moment. He stepped closer, searching every line in Jacob's wrinkled face. Then he stepped back. Slowly he said in broken German, "Ich bin der Christli Hochstetler" (I am Christian Hochstetler).

—E. Stoll

Division between the Old Orders and the Progressives

The Amish in America lived in unity for many generations. But by the 1850s, there was tension between different settlements and within settlements. New things were creeping in. The camera had been invented, and some Amish were having family photographs taken. Young men were beginning to wear neckties, and other customs in dress were changing. The ban was not strictly enforced in some congregations. Some ministers were discarding prayer books. Insurance was catching on among the "English," and some Amish were interested and subscribed to the plan. A few congregations wondered if it wouldn't be better to baptize in running water.

In 1851, David Beiler, a well-known and strict bishop of Lancaster County, Pennsylvania, wrote a letter to Moses B. Miller, the bishop at Johnstown, Pennsylvania: "I have often been thinking that a general ministers' meeting is needed, so we could admonish each other orally with love, in a humble spirit, with Christian simplicity, so that nobody would insist on his own opinion, but take the Word of the Lord as a guide."

A general ministers' meeting (*Diener-Versammlung*) was not held until eleven years after David Beiler made his suggestion. Meanwhile, another problem arose among the Amish churches—the question of meetinghouses. A small log meetinghouse had been built in 1830 by the Amish in Stark County, Ohio, and a small frame one in 1848 in the Clinton district in Elkhart County, Indiana.

Actually, the first Amish meetinghouse in America had been erected as early as 1795 in Chester County, Pennsylvania, but the settlement had become extinct within a generation. No other eastern Amish settlement followed the example of the Chester County Amish.

The first general ministers' meeting was held in June of 1862 in Wayne County, Ohio. Some strict Amish bishops attended the sessions. But from studying in which communities the meetings were held and who the chairmen were, it is obvious that from the beginning the meetings were under the control of the progressive Amish bishops, not the stricter ones. Instead of the ministers' meetings being an aid in stopping drift in the Amish church, it opened the door and let the changes in.

A year later, in May of 1863, the second general ministers' meeting was held. For the next fifteen years, they continued to be held annually, except in 1877.

The final general ministers' meeting was held in 1878 in Woodford County, Illinois. After that session, the ministers decided to discontinue the meetings. They saw that the meetings were failing to restore unity among the Amish in America. By this time, the stricter bishops had given up hope of holding the progressive ones back. And the progressive bishops had grown tired of being reminded of "the old way."

The meetings had begun in 1862 with the hope of arriving at new unity, but the only new unity reached was among the progressive bishops. They soon formed three regional conferences of their own. Altogether, there were approximately seventy congregations. They no longer referred to themselves simply as Amish, but adopted the term *Amish Mennonite*, which was very fitting, for they were a church between the Amish and the Mennonites.

It has been estimated that two-thirds of the Amish in America went with this liberal movement, the other third remaining Amish and calling themselves Old Order Amish. The Amish Mennonites continued to change, and by 1927 nearly all the congregations had dropped the term *Amish* and had united with the Mennonite church.

—D. Luthy

Amish Life in the Great Depression, 1930–40
Nappanee, Indiana, by Joni D. Gingerich

[Summary:] Joni was married in 1929. He worked in a lamp and chair shop until it went out of business in 1930. Joni had no job the rest of the 1930 winter. March 1931 brought a child, and no income from the summer. In May, he worked on a farm nine miles away for a dollar a day, house and garden rent-free, and pasture for driving horse and cow.

The next year he rented this farm. He followed sales and eventually bought some farm implements, a team of horses, seven milk cows, a few breed sows, some hay and grain. Joni had no manure spreader, so he hauled it in a wagon and spread it by hand twice a week. He planted thirty acres of corn and twelve of soybeans. Non-Amish and Amish helped with some work.

Joni had no money or income that summer, so he couldn't buy groceries. He took a bushel of shelled corn to the milling company to be ground into cornmeal. Thirty-five cents or half the corn was the price. He paid half the corn. Then he bought a bushel of wheat and had half of it ground coarse for cereal, and half of it fine for bread. "That was the main diet around our place for a number of years—whole wheat cereal, whole wheat pudding, mush and milk, fried mush, corn bread, and potatoes. We ate that for three meals a day, seven days a week."

He hired a Mennonite man who needed money for his family for a week. The man asked for $1.25 a day, besides food that the Amishman had sent him. The man said another man offered him that much, but it turned out it was a trick to get more money.

Joni feels that lessons were learned and that some young people could benefit from a taste of such hard times. He also asks, "Could it be that we are in a greater depression spiritual-wise than we were back there money-wise?"

Belleville, Pennsylvania, by Jonathan R. Byler Sr.

"As for myself and family, the Depression taught lessons not soon forgotten. It was sometimes hard to tell one's life companion how little money was at hand, especially when clothing and so forth were needed. But being farmers, we usually had plenty to eat. Faith in God and honesty were a great help. I doubt if anyone can know the mercy God has bestowed upon mankind since the beginning of time."

Lancaster, Pennsylvania, by Jonathan Zook

"We were married December 5, 1918, and started farming and housekeeping in the spring of 1919. We had good years until the year of 1930. Around May or June, as nearly as I can tell, the bottom seemed to drop out of everything.

"That spring we had torn down our old barn (116 years old) and were building a new one. The carpenters had charged

65 cents an hour, which was a good wage then. But that fall when we built a chicken house, their price had dropped to 35 cents an hour. By 1931, most building stopped altogether. Carpenters were glad if they could find work at 25 cents. Many contractors went broke because they had new houses on hand at high prices and could not sell them.

"Farmers also had a tough job of making ends meet. If we broke even till the end of the year, we were well satisfied. Hogs sold for 2 cents a pound, steers 4.5 cents a pound, potatoes 25 cents a bushel, and milk 80 cents a hundred. In 1934, it got better. About 1936, things leveled off, and supply and demand took care of themselves. In 1939–40, when Hitler in Germany started to invade countries, prices started to rise, and have risen ever since.

"During the Depression, church members needed one another, and church affairs went along nicely. But now things have changed because there is so much money that comes easily and buys so many worldly things."

Pennsylvania Dutch: "Kannscht du Deitsch schwetze?" [Can You Speak Dutch?]

"What is Pennsylvania Dutch, anyway, and where does it come from?"

Sometimes people refer to Pennsylvania Dutch as "poor German with English words mixed into it." Others refer to it as "Low German." High German is called "high" because it is spoken in the mountainous or higher regions of Germany, whereas Low German is spoken in the lower parts.

Pennsylvania Dutch may be an inaccurate label since it isn't "Dutch" at all [the term *Deitsch* (*Dutch*) came from *Deutsch*, meaning "German"]. But the word *Pennsylvania* is accurate since the dialect is deeply rooted in that state. When William

Penn offered his colony of Pennsylvania as a haven for persecuted religious minorities, many people moved there. The Mennonites, Amish, and Brethren Dunkards were early settlers. They emigrated from the Palatinate, a region in southern Germany. They also came from Baden, Württemberg, Hesse, and Bavaria—also regions in southern Germany. Some came from Alsace and Switzerland. They were known as the Plain people because of their unadorned dress and simple lives.

At the same time that the Plain people moved to Pennsylvania, other emigrants from the exact same areas moved there too. They came more for financial reasons than because of persecution. They belonged to Lutheran, Catholic, and Reformed churches. They became known as the "gay" Dutch, as opposed to the "plain" Dutch.

One thing that the settlers shared in common, whether "gay" or "plain," was the German language. They all spoke a German dialect, but not the same dialect. As they lived side by side in the southeastern counties of Pennsylvania, their dialects gradually blended to form what we today call Pennsylvania Dutch.

Since the largest number of settlers had come from the Palatinate, the German dialect of that region (*pfälzisch*) became the foundation upon which the Pennsylvania Dutch dialect was built. Nevertheless, the Pennsylvania Dutch dialect does not match 100 percent any dialect in Germany. It is a true German dialect that developed in America rather than in Germany.

Since the Amish trace back to the Swiss Brethren in Canton Bern, Switzerland, the dialect of their forebears was *Berndeutsch*. Today, it is commonly referred to in Amish circles as *Schweizer Deitsch* (Swiss German). The Amish who live in Adams and Allen Counties, Indiana, have rather well retained this native Amish dialect. But they are so in the minority today that their speech is looked upon by other Amish as odd.

Professor Albert Buffington of Lancaster County, Pennsylvania, has studied the Pennsylvania Dutch dialect. He estimates that 2 to 8 percent of the dialect is made up of English words. Since the national language in America is English, and since Amish are educated in that language, it is only natural that new words that enter Pennsylvania Dutch will be English. Words differ from one settlement to the next, and so does the tone of voice and the accent. It has been estimated that there are half a million people in North America who can converse freely in the dialect, and another half a million who can understand it.

—D. Luthy

What Is in a Language?

English is the language of our country. But we, the descendants of immigrants from German-speaking parts of Europe, have clung to a language that has become largely our own. Over the years that our people have lived alongside English-speaking neighbors, we have naturally and gradually accepted numerous English words into our German dialect. The Pennsylvania Dutch we speak is really a slowly changing language. It is somewhat different now than it was a hundred years ago, and it is not even exactly the same in different parts of the country. Our case is much like that of the Jews in New Testament times.

The Old Testament was first written almost entirely in the old Hebrew language. It was the language of the Jews until the time of their captivity in the far-off land of Babylon. In that land [a faithful remnant] kept the faith better than the Israelites had during any other time in their history. But by the time they returned to their homeland, most of the people talked a different dialect called Aramaic. Then later, by the time the books that now make up the New Testament were written, roughly between the years AD 50–100, another language had worked its way up to become the chief language of commerce in the land of the Jews, and in most of the lands of that part of the world. That language was [Koine] Greek.

Thus the case of the people at that time was much like ours today. They had the traditional Hebrew for their worship just as we use the German Bible in our homes and churches. They had the Aramaic, a language spoken in their homes, but hardly popular as a written language at that time, much as we use our everyday Pennsylvania Dutch. Then for their writings and correspondence, they had the common Greek, the easy-to-write language of world commerce and business, somewhat similar to the way we use the English language in our day.

Knowing two languages is a privilege that God has provided for us, and we can put them to good use. Although we have a knowledge of two languages, it would be wrong not to make an effort to express ourselves better in the English language. But it would be just as wrong to fail to keep and pass on the German to our children—that rich language our forebears left for us. It is a well-known fact that losing our mother tongue and drifting into the world usually go together.

Anytime we speak English around the home when just family members are around, or while working or visiting with others who know Pennsylvania Dutch, we put in a vote to drop a rich heritage that will never again be brought back if we lose it.

The value of that heritage is so great that we can't afford to lose it.

—Staff

THREE

Choices

MANY OF US SEE THE AMISH RELIGION and lifestyle merely as a complex series of rules to be followed. We have difficulty understanding why certain things are allowed, while others are not. As outsiders, we have questions about why photographs are forbidden, why there are so many particulars on how to dress, and so on.

Many Amish themselves cannot answer these questions, beyond a simple "We've always done it that way." Yet little that the Amish practice is done simply by whim. In the pages of *Family Life*, there are many attempts to explore, explain, and even debate the reasons behind practices that have or may become Amish customs and traditions.

The Heritage of Our Church Decisions

Our Amish churches everywhere use rules of conduct, or *Ordnung*, to maintain uniformity in the church, and to keep unwanted practices out of the church. There are people who label all such as man-made rules, and say they are wrong and detrimental to the church. But we believe that one of the points which has enabled the Amish to hold to nonconformity is discipline. To have discipline, we must have standards. If we rebel against the standards decided by the church, it is evident that something is wrong in our heart.

Each restriction we have is the result of some problem or misuse the church faced at one time. When we face new problems, we must make decisions whether we want to act on them or not. When I was a boy, there was no rule against watching or owning a television set, for the simple reason that there was no television. A hundred years ago the church needed no *Ordnung* against short dresses because at that time it was the practice among all women to wear them floor length.

For myself, I prefer to go by the collective decisions that have been made and handed down to us over many generations. Is there not a real danger that if we throw out what we have inherited from our forebears, we may be missing something we will not be able to replace?

—D. Wagler

Convicting the Hearers

Many members know the church rules better than the scriptural basis for them. I firmly believe fewer young people would be lost to the alluring world if their parents and ministers made sure they knew the biblical foundation of their beliefs instead of merely telling them that is how the church teaches. It is harder to turn your back on "Thus saith the Lord" than on "Thus saith the church."

—Anonymous

What It Means to Be Amish

We dress differently and our lifestyle is different, but is that the only difference between the Amish and all these other churches?

Well, let me tell you a story. Some years ago a group of fifty-two people chartered a bus and came to Holmes County to see the Amish. They had arranged to have an Amishman meet them and answer some of their questions.

For their first question, they began, "We all go to church," and named some churches. "So we know about Jesus. But what does it mean to be Amish?"

The Amishman thought a bit, and then he asked a question of his own. "How many of you have television in your homes?" Fifty-two hands went up. "Now, how many of you feel that perhaps you would be better off without television in your homes?" Again, fifty-two hands went up. "All right. Now, how many of you are going to go home and get rid of your television?" Not one hand went up!

Now that is what it means to be Amish. As a church, if we see or experience something that is not good for us spiritually, we will discipline ourselves to do without.

The world in general does not know what it is to do without!

—Monroe L. Beachy

The World Is Changing

No longer do people want to stay at home and live a quiet and godly life. They must be going, going, going, running after pleasure. The automobile opens the way.

Some think that doing missionary work is the answer. They must go and help people in foreign countries. They do not stop to think that staying at home and being a good example to the neighbors is also doing missionary work. Too often those who go to foreign lands must hear the words "Physician, heal thyself."

I don't mean that missionary work is wrong, but it seems that our first responsibility is to our family. We can also witness to the people around us. But it seems the people in the world today want to have the church salve their conscience, and they still want to keep the things they crave.

Many will probably say, "Someone is always crying wolf." But the truth is that the wolf of worldliness is at our door and ready to devour the sheep.

—L. S.

Prayers and Publicans

There are at least two ways we can get into the mistake of being self-righteous—through insincere prayer, and through bragging about our goodness. If these were the only two ways that self-righteousness showed itself, most of us would be pretty safe. As Amish, we don't have prayer meetings or testimony services, two places where these types of self-righteousness seem especially likely to be present. But this surely does not mean that we are free from self-righteousness.

For example, it is easy to see that those in higher [more liberal, progressive] churches are wrong to have the attitude of "God, I thank thee that I am not like those Old Order people!" But is it possible that the same self-righteous spirit could make us say the prayer in reverse: "God, I thank thee that I am not like those people in the higher churches!"

To be self-righteously proud is wrong, always wrong, even though the things we are proud of may be right in themselves. It is right that we wear plain clothes, drive horses, live separate from the world, have our own schools, and things like that. But just as soon as we become proud about any of these things, we will be condemned right along with the self-righteous Pharisee (Luke 18:9-14).

Self-righteousness is such a sly sin. We need to be alert, watch for it daily, and humble ourselves whenever we have become exalted. Even then we cannot relax, for what is easier to be proud of than of the fact that we are so humble?

—E. Stoll

Cars and Tractors

The Danger of Horsepower

"He shall not multiply horses to himself" (Deuteronomy 17:16).

We are not conformed to this world. That includes our dress, but it surely also includes our way of making a living. We can believe that it also includes our way of traveling on the road, and our way of working in our fields. What means of travel today is highly esteemed among men? Which means of travel today corresponds with what horses stood for in Bible times?

Our neighbor may pass us on the road with all that "horsepower" under the hood. He works his fields with machinery that has so much more "horsepower" than we are using. Nevertheless, let us be content to stay with our work in a small, honest, and humble way, and not multiply horses to ourselves.

—An Amish minister

Traveling Time

Shallow reasoning has been used by people who decided it didn't make sense to spend an hour going to town by buggy when they could go the same distance by car in ten minutes. "Why," such people have reasoned, "if we had a car, we wouldn't spend nearly as much time on the road and could be at home with the family more."

By taking one single trip to town and figuring how much longer it would take by buggy, the above conclusion sounds reasonable. But the matter isn't that simple. Instead of spending less time on the road, people who switch to motorized transportation soon discover they are on the road more than before.

Since it's easier to go to town, they tend to go oftener and for smaller needs. They soon begin to shop and visit places farther from home. It's just as easy to drive fifty miles as it used to be to drive five, and that's exactly what they do. So they end up spending more time on the road than before.

—E. Stoll

Telephones: The Choice of Two Evils

"I wonder which is the worst, anyway?" Fred Hostetler muttered to himself as he sat down at the supper table.

"Worst of what?" his wife, Saloma, asked as she stirred a pinch of salt into the soup.

"I mean, which way would be the worst, to have a phone of our own, or to be continually pestering our neighbors to use theirs?"

"Surely you don't think we should get telephones?" Saloma asked as a frown crossed her face. "Our people have never had them. You wouldn't want to change the *Ordnung* now, would you?"

"No, I wouldn't," Fred answered firmly. "But just the same, I still can't help wondering sometimes which would be the worst. Did you know that they allowed telephones over in the Concordia settlement?"

"You mean there where Atlee Kauffmans moved? I knew they were a little more liberal in some things, but I never thought they would allow telephones."

"They figured it would be a better light to the world to have telephones than to be bothering their neighbors all the time to use theirs."

"But couldn't they explain why we don't have telephones?"

"I guess so, but I've found it's harder to explain that to someone than it is to explain why we don't have cars or radios or something like that," Fred said. "Atlee wrote that the phones are to be allowed strictly for business and emergency only, no gossiping or unnecessary calling."

About five years later, Fred Hostetlers were planning a trip to visit close relatives in Missouri. "Why don't we stop at Concordia on the way back and visit Atlee Kauffmans?" Fred asked.

The Kauffmans were glad to see their old neighbors and welcomed them warmly. "You just come in and sit down. You can visit until dinner is ready," Ruby Kauffman said.

Fred went out to see Atlee, who was remodeling the cow stable. As the men walked from the barn toward the pasture, a shrill voice came from the house, "Dad-dy! Telephone!"

When Atlee returned, he grumbled, "Those seed corn agents can sure be a nuisance. I told him the other day I'd let him know if I wanted to order anything from him. But he insists on calling me every few days."

After showing Fred around the farm a bit, Atlee said, "We may just as well go in. Dinner should be ready in an hour."

They washed up and went to sit down in the living room. Fred thought he heard a conversation going on, and then saw that Ruby was talking on the telephone. As the men came into the room, she was saying, "Well, I'll have to go now. We've got company for dinner. Thanks for calling. I'll call you back later."

They sat down to visit, and Atlee started telling how his team of horses ran away the summer before. "We let them stand in the hayfield, and they got scared of the baler. Up the lane they went toward home as fast as they could go, until they got to that tree in the lane. Then one horse went around on one side of the tree, and the other one on the other side, and the wagon—"

"Rrrrrr!" The ring of the phone interrupted the story. Atlee came back and took up the conversation where he had left off. After some time, the phone rang again. Atlee answered it: "Yes, yes. Who? Minerva? Yes, she's here."

About this time the oldest daughter came flying into the room and grabbed the receiver. From the kitchen came the voice of Ruby as she lamented, "Minerva wouldn't have to get so excited every time the phone rings. Now she went and spilled the cornstarch all over the work table. Those Worner girls have a bad habit of calling her any time of the day."

Fred and Atlee got back into their conversation. At eleven thirty, Ruby came into the room, picked up the receiver, and started dialing. "Hello, Patty. This is me. I hate to bother you, but right now I discovered we're plum out of sugar. We forgot to get some the other day when we were in town. We need some to make the frosting on the cake."

By the time dinner was ready, it was just past twelve o'clock. Ruby had fixed a big meal, and everyone was hungry. As the family sat down to the table, everyone bowed their heads solemnly to give thanks to the almighty God in heaven for his goodness in providing such a bounteous meal. Just as everyone had folded their hands and silently bowed their heads, there was a loud noise. "Rrrrrrr!" The telephone was urgently ringing . . .

As the big Greyhound bus pulled into the station, the Hostetlers hastily bade goodbye to their friends. Soon they were on the last stretch of their journey, heading home.

"Are you still wondering what it would be like to have a telephone in the house?" Saloma asked.

Fred almost had to smile as he answered. "Well, now I know what it could be like, but that's not saying it would have to be like that. I don't think everyone with a telephone has as much going on as the Kauffmans did."

"That could all be," Saloma agreed. "But actually, you only saw half of it. In the afternoon when you and Atlee went over to visit old Sam Miller, the phone was as busy as ever. One time Ruby called Allen Kauffman's wife to ask how much soda she puts in her coconut cookies. Then later in the afternoon, she called her sister to ask what number of thread she uses to sew that blue double-knit material for a dress. That time she talked for about half an hour. And Minerva, I think she called up her friends and talked with them several times during the afternoon. She seems to have a lot of friends of all kinds. Are you still unable to answer your question?"

"It looks to me like that would be making a choice between two evils, and I don't think it is necessary to do either one. What I had in mind was the way they do it out in Missouri, but I don't believe that's the perfect answer either."

"How do they do it there?"

"They asked the telephone company to put a phone at the schoolhouse. It's not a large community there, and they can go to the schoolhouse to do their calling. Then they don't have to bother their neighbors so much. They seem to think it's working out all right, and as far as bothering the neighbors is concerned, it apparently is. But I'm afraid there's another danger they may not realize."

"What's that?"

"I'm afraid they're using the phone more than they really have to," Fred said. "By planning their business out ahead, they could often get along without using the phone as they do now. From what I saw in Missouri, I think they could have done a lot of their business by mail, such as ordering feed, and so on."

"But wouldn't it be handier to do it by phone?" Saloma asked.

"Yes, it would be, and sometimes it is about the only way it can be done," Fred agreed. "But a lot of other things would be handy too. What I was wondering is, Will their children be able to see the dangers in having these things which are so handy, if the parents make use of them so much as they do?"

"I guess there's a danger any way you do it," Saloma said. "But do you mean to say that out there in Missouri, they never have to bother their neighbors?"

"I never said that," Fred answered. "There will still be emergencies, such as someone getting hurt, when they want to get help as soon as possible. I don't think the neighbors object to using their phones at times like that. It's the idea of bothering them continually and for things that don't look necessary to them. That's what gets on their nerves."

"I don't think I'd appreciate that myself," Saloma responded.

"I guess not," Fred laughed, "especially if they tracked their dirty boots over your nice clean floor right after you had done the Saturday cleaning!"

—Anonymous

Issues

Following are short articles of discussion and debate on a variety of issues. A question is often posed in the "What Do You Think?" column, and readers send in their thoughts.

Vaccinations

Does vaccination show a lack of faith in God?

[Four of the five answers felt vaccinations were acceptable. The one negative response considered it a form of insurance. One writer said it is common to vaccinate horses, cattle, and hogs, so why not children? Another reader responded:]

Yes, I strongly feel it's our duty to protect our children from disease when it's in our power. People who say we shouldn't vaccinate remind me of the man who was sitting in his buggy with his horse hitched up. When someone told him there was a child standing between the buggy wheels, he answered, "Oh, just trust in God. He'll take care of the child."

I don't think such attitudes are right. We should do our part, and do what we can.

—Anonymous

Social Security

We have asked to be exempt from Social Security so we won't become dependent on the government. Many of our people signed statements: "I am conscientiously opposed on religious grounds, as taught in Matthew 6:34, to old age and survivors' insurance. I want to put my trust in our heavenly Father for my future needs, as stated in Matthew 6:31-33 and Psalm 37:7-25. Should I, through sickness or otherwise, become in need, rather than accept government benefits, I trust that I will be taken care of through my respected church with alms, as has been our practice since before our people came to America and to this day." Every year through alms, thousands of dollars are used to help our old and needy. Yet I fear that in the future, more of our Amish people will show up at government institutions unless we can make provisions for our love, dollars, and hands to help share their burdens.

—Anonymous

Hunting and Owning Guns

The Amish have traditionally used guns to hunt for food and have not had a conscience against it. I am sixty years old and cannot remember that the practice was ever questioned until a few years ago.

Last fall one of my brothers, older than I, shot a deer on his farm and provided himself with a nice supply of meat for the winter. I think the deer is a lovely creature, and I doubt if anyone gets more pleasure out of watching them trot through the bottoms on a summer day. On the other hand, their meat is so similar to beef that I cannot believe they were created just to look at.

For myself, I can see no connection between owning a gun and nonresistance, or between shooting a rabbit and killing a person. Sometimes it's the misuse of a thing that's wrong and not the thing itself. I think there is a big difference between the man who hunts rabbit or squirrel or deer for food, and the one who goes to Wyoming to hunt elk for sport.

—Anonymous

Games and Sports

To what degree is it proper for us to take part in sports and games played within our own communities? Here there does not appear to be easy agreement.

In some communities, married men go to town and play baseball, an Amish team against a non-Amish team. Other communities would frown on that, but would think nothing of married men playing, as long as both teams were made up of members of the Amish community.

Then in still other communities, the married men would not play, but boys with the young folks would play ball Sunday afternoons after church services. Other communities would not permit their young people to play on Sunday, but their young people, both boys and girls, would gather to play ball during the week.

Last of all, some communities teach that playing should be confined to children, and sports to the world. Such communities feel that neither game playing nor sports are fitting for church members, whether married or unmarried.

Amid such variation, where is the correct place to make a line? To complicate matters, ball playing is only one example. The same questions apply to hunting and fishing, racing horses,

volleyball, hockey, card playing, and all other games adults play.
I will attempt to state my own personal convictions:

1. Playing is for children. It is not wrong for parents to guide
   and instruct their children in wholesome play; nor is it
   wrong for parents to join children in play at suitable times.
   But it does seem out of place when adults spend time
   playing games with each other.

2. Sports belong to the world.

3. Games promote a generation gap. Some parents have tried
   to overcome this by advocating that married people should
   join in freely with games and sports of the young people.
   I, for one, would be unspeakably ashamed if the judgment
   day should dawn suddenly and find me, along with the
   rest of the church (bishop, fellow ministers, parents, young
   people) playing a game of volleyball.

4. Sports break down our separation [from the world].

5. Sports detract from worthwhile things.

6. Sports destroy a sense of modesty.

7. Sports fail to satisfy.

8. Games are disrespectful on Sunday. If we have any purpose
   in life at all, any spiritual goals we seek to obtain, we
   should surely be able one day out of the entire week to find
   something worthwhile to occupy our time and attention.

—E. Stoll

Law and Order

Someone asks, "Should a Christian call or notify the police after he finds his home broken into or burglarized while away
from home? Does calling the police go against the teaching of
nonresistance?"

You wonder how far defenseless Christians should go when thieves enter their house. Inform the police about what took place and answer their questions. That's it. No charges. No prosecution if the thieves are caught. Paul urges Christians to give civil authorities their due, be it in taxes, respect, or honor (Romans 13:1-7; Titus 3:1). We should always make sure there is *no* money left at home whenever we go away. Let us not be found guilty of leading weaker souls into temptation.

—Anonymous

For Complete Separation

After reading the answers on notifying police in cases of theft, I did some thinking. A nonresistant person cannot have someone else using force for him or through his cooperation. If a thief is caught, the person who reported him is helping to bring punishment upon him. Wouldn't we be like Pilate? He saw "no fault" in Jesus but gave in to Jewish leaders, washing his own hands to signify innocence. Yet in our eyes, Pilate still shares the guilt [since he sentenced Jesus to be crucified; Matthew 27; Luke 23].

Separation of church and state should be complete. We should not use the state for our own purposes, but deny officials when they demand our assistance, such as in armed service or alternative duties. To submit to the government, as we are admonished in 1 Peter 2:13, doesn't mean pulling in the harness with them, but just to obey them as far as our conscience allows.

—Anonymous

Church and State

This question of what our responsibility is to the government can indeed be a difficult one, and for many areas besides whether or not to report crimes. Recently I happened to be talking with a neighbor who is not of a Plain background, but still a professing Christian. He asked me what I thought of capital punishment. That is not an easy question. I never did get it explained so that he was satisfied. He said I was trying to both agree and disagree with it, and that was impossible. The root of the problem was that he could not understand our concept of separation of church and state.

I tried to explain to him that as a Christian, I could not punish anyone or take revenge, much less take a person's life. Jesus taught his followers to forgive and turn the other cheek. That was my position and the position of our church.

However, that is not what God ordained for the government. The Lord ordained government to protect the good and punish the evil [Romans 13]. The government's role is based on the old Mosaic Law of justice—eye for eye, tooth for tooth [Exodus 21:23-25]. Therefore, I did not condemn capital punishment for the government, as long as every attempt is made to fulfill [the law] in justice.

My neighbor shakes his head and tells me I should make up my mind: either something is good or it is bad; either say yes or no. But this is not a matter of indecision. Instead, I have a firm conviction that the role of the government is different from that of the church. And the two must be forever separate. It is yes for one, but no for the other.

—Staff

Voting

I don't feel Christians should take part in voting for those who seek government office. If we do vote for such persons and help them get into office, we would also be indirectly responsible for their deeds, such as acts of war and so forth. We ought to obey God rather than man [Acts 5:29].

The Bible does teach us to pray for those who rule over us [1 Timothy 2:1-2]. We should not take part in worldly affairs. This, I believe, is or can lead to the downfall of our Plain churches.

—A. H.

One may perhaps argue that Christians who live in America or Canada live in a democracy, a free country, and hence are duty bound to take part in the voting process and otherwise support such a government system. Our government does indeed protect and defend our right to worship God freely and in whatever manner we wish. However, as good as any country may be to live in, both Canadian and American systems of government are still much a part of this world. And in James 1:27, we read that pure and undefiled religion means to keep oneself unstained from the world.

Just because a great many Christians do participate in the voting process doesn't necessarily make it right. The Scriptures nowhere encourage one to take part in any governmental system that is part of the world. And in voting, one would in a small way be doing just this.

—Anonymous

Labor Unions: All We Need Is Your Signature

I am replying to your request for me to join the union [where I work]. I have talked it over with several of my brethren in Christ and also with one of our ministers. None of them felt that it would be a benefit for me or to the church if I joined the union. I will try to state our reasons for not joining.

First, we as Christians must stand out from the world by the way we dress and act. In 1 Peter 2:9, we read, "But you are a chosen generation, a royal priesthood, an holy nation, a peculiar people; that you should show forth the praises of him who has called you out of darkness into his marvelous light."

In James 1:27, we read that pure religion is [to keep ourselves] unspotted from the world. (We don't have cars, radios, television, electricity, musical instruments, telephones, stereos, and things like that.)

Then in 2 Corinthians 6:14, Paul says we should not be unequally yoked with unbelievers. I'm not saying that everyone in the union is an unbeliever, but some are. By signing up I would surely be yoking myself with unbelievers. Nowhere in the Bible have I been able to find that we as Christians should join any club or organization except the church of God.

We don't think that everything the union does is bad. But they have made the news a number of times lately with their acts of violence and lawlessness. In Ohio, I understand that just recently, members of the truckers union killed several persons. It is true that I can join the union and still not help to do things like that. But I feel that if I join the union, then I will be held partly responsible for what they do since I know beforehand that they do things like this. This is the way I look at it: I can't hold the gun and be innocent of the shooting just because I let someone else pull the trigger.

Generally speaking, we feel that the union's way of dealing with the company is directly contrary to the true Christian way. The union says to the company, "You pay us so-and-so or else," but the Bible teaches us to recompense no man evil for evil [Romans 12:17]. We are to love our enemies, bless them that curse us, do good to them that hate us, and pray for those who despitefully use us (Matthew 5:44).

In other words, the union uses force, but the Bible teaches us to use love and good works. In our church, we don't try to force anyone to join, but we do try to use our influence so that people will want to join. I believe the union should work the same way.

Last, though I am in perfect agreement with the church in their stand against labor unions, I would still not go against my religious convictions. If I have a job a union member wants, I will exchange jobs with him, and I will not vote against the union. But I think you should have an exemption in your contract for people whose faith keeps them from joining your union.

I do not have any ill feelings against you or anyone else in the union. If there are any more questions, I will be glad to try to answer them for you.

—Anonymous

Photographs

A question was raised about having knickknacks, dolls, and photographs, since Exodus 20:4 seems to forbid them.

No Graven Image

Perhaps it is time for us Plain people to examine our position concerning pictures and photographs. Why do we feel as we do?

When we Plain people are asked why we are opposed to the use of photographs, someone often comes up with the verse from Exodus 20, the second of the Ten Commandments: "Thou shalt not make unto thee any graven image, or any likeness of any thing that is in heaven above, or that is in the earth beneath, or that is in the water under the earth."

However, does this verse really fit when applied to having our picture taken? The answer is neither a simple yes or no, or perhaps it is both.

If we mean in a literal way, the answer is no. The verse does not apply because the verse says we should not make a graven image or a likeness of anything, period. It doesn't say, "Thou shalt not make a photograph of a man's face, but to trace the outline of a child's foot is all right." Of course, we make likenesses in many other ways. Taken literally, the verse would not allow us to draw a blueprint of a house, our children should not make a picture to color, and *Family Life* shouldn't print a picture on its cover.

Or does the verse just mean photographs taken with a camera? We still have problems. Does that mean we wouldn't object to having our portrait painted, which often looks nearly as true to life as a photo? Does it mean we shouldn't permit X-rays to be taken, which are photographs of internal parts of our bodies? If pictures of people's faces are wrong, why do we use things with such pictures every day, on our money and coins, and on our postage stamps?

So if we answer in a literal and direct way, we would have to say no, the second commandment is not talking about taking snapshots. (If it were, what were the poor people supposed to make of it for the thousands of years before the comparatively recent invention of the camera?)

Maybe someone will say Exodus 20:4 means a graven image, a likeness carved or molded, with a three-dimensional effect. But that wouldn't even include photographs. Besides, we don't observe the graven-image part, either. Check how many toy cows and horses are in your child's toy box.

However, if it is understood in an indirect way, yes, the Plain people's traditional opposition to photographs and their tendency to be camera shy can be connected with the commandment against idolatry. Taken in this indirect way, some of the things that appear inconsistent in our stand begin to make sense. That will then explain why we are not alarmed by the toy cow in the play box, the picture on the postage stamp, but try to look the other way when someone holds a camera in front of us.

We believe that posing for photographs is part of the world's misguided emphasis on glorifying the outward person. The Bible tells us that it is the inner man that is important [1 Peter 3:3-4]. Fixing up our hair, wearing jewelry, bright colors, fancy clothing—these are the world's ways of drawing attention to the beauty of the created. God wants us to honor the Creator, not the created. The world puts a lot of emphasis on a pretty girl or a handsome boy. As Christians, we should work against this kind of thinking. A person's facial features should not affect our opinion of a person's worth or value.

Thus we believe that letting ourselves get involved in the world of photography leads us away from humility, not toward true humility. We already have problems with too much emphasis on dress and finery at weddings and such occasions. Going to a photo studio to have such occasions recorded in a permanent visual record only increases this temptation toward false values and unchristian adornment. We have enough pride in our hearts without feeding and encouraging it by doing things that tend to increase the temptations.

There is also the stewardship question. Photography is expensive. Once a church becomes involved in it, there seems to be no end to the sums that can be spent for equipment and film. All this to attempt and make permanent what God has decreed shall pass away.

In conclusion, then, if we take the second commandment directly and literally, it doesn't make sense to apply it to our opposition to cameras. But taken in a more indirect way, things begin to add up. We don't want to emphasize the outer self, lest we do it at the expense of the inner being. We don't want to exalt self, lest we rob the Creator of his glory.

It follows, then, that we are not opposed to a graven image in the toy box; few people are tempted to hang their hearts on a child's toy. That explains why we make a difference between a photograph of our backbone and one of our faces. No proud grandfather has been tempted to impress people he meets by pulling from his wallet X-ray photos of his grandchild's spinal column! (This is also why some church groups allow snapshots to be taken when requested by the government for their files, photos not kept personally.)

No, let us not slip gradually, bit by bit, into the ways of the world that lead to an emphasis on pride and personal vanity. When we are gone, let us be remembered not by the breadth of our noses, the height of our brows, or the angle of our cheekbones, but by what truly matters—the lives we have lived and the examples we have left. Dust we are, to dust we shall return [Genesis 3:19]. Why frame and embellish and hang on the wall the pictures of this house of clay in which we live? Let us beware lest we permit self to be exalted, becoming unto us a graven image.

—E. Stoll

A Spoiled Generation

Several years ago I noticed a small cartoon in a newspaper that caught my attention. It showed a picture of a living room in a typical modern home. A brightly lit and gaily decorated Christmas tree was in one corner. A ten-year-old boy stood in the middle of a wide assortment of toys he had just unwrapped. There was an electric train piled to one side of him, a brand-new bike leaning against the wall, a catcher's mitt at his feet, and a model airplane in his hands. The room all around him was strewn with expensive toys and gifts and wrapping paper.

It was a simple cartoon, but it told a complete story. He held the last gift in his hand and was looking around for more, with a frown on his face. Under the cartoon was the caption "You mean this is all I get?"

What a spoiled child! His parents had spent a couple hundred dollars on several dozen toys, gadgets, and playthings. Instead of being awed and grateful, he complained because there wasn't more. Instead of complaining, his eyes should have been shining and his lips saying, "You mean I get all this!"

However hard it is to believe that a child could be so spoiled, the truth is that all of us have more in common with this child than we like to think. In a way, all of us have become spoiled children, unbelievably blessed in material things, yet standing amid plenty and waste and asking, "You mean this is all I get?"

We have life rather easy compared with our forebears. They were hunted, persecuted, tortured, and killed. The government passed special laws against them. We have religious freedom, and the government passes special laws in our favor. [We don't expect to suffer] torture or pain [as punishment for faith].

Our immigrant forefathers toiled with their axes and hoes to wrest a living from thick forests and tree-stump-covered clearings. We have rich dark soil, loose and fertile and productive, and teams of horses to work it with. They had to make almost everything, from their ax handles to their homespun clothing. We go to town and buy what we want. No weary hours working into the night carving, weaving, spinning.

Our forebears had a diet with little variety—corn mush, potatoes, meat. Our tables are loaded with delicacies they never heard of—bananas, oranges, and pineapples. They wore clothing that was rough, stiff, and uncomfortable. We have super fabrics with nylon added to last longer, or Dacron to keep out the wrinkles.

We have it easy. We have grown fat, soft, lazy, and spoiled. We have forgotten how to suffer, and we refuse even to be inconvenienced. Everything has to be handy. Our ancestors would walk several hundred miles to visit relatives. They would ride horseback over rough and dangerous trails, taking several weeks or months to make the trip. Today, Greyhound buses speeding over superhighways aren't fast enough for us. We want a taxi to pick us up at our doorstep and chauffeur us wherever we want to go. It's too much bother to change buses, carry suitcases, and wait in depots. Will our children in turn find it too much bother to hire a taxi, and decide to buy a car themselves so they can go when and where they like?

It does seem to work that way. The luxuries of one generation become the necessities of the next. Let's look at just one area of life, our water supply. When our forebears came to this country, they likely carried their water from a spring. There were many trips for water, morning, evenings, and even throughout the day. It was tiresome, time-consuming labor, but it was accepted without question because it had to be done.

Gradually, as homes became more permanent, wells became common. What a luxury this must have seemed! A well within a hundred feet of the house. No more long trips down the dusty, winding path for water. Now it was close, convenient, and handy. All they had to do was lower the bucket into the well, and hand over hand pull up sparkling, clean, fresh water.

After a generation or two, pumps came on the scene. Ah, once again, how handy it seemed. No more straining backs and tired, aching arms, pulling that rope to bring up a bucket of water. Just grab the pump handle, and up comes the water. It was much quicker and easier.

Nevertheless, what one generation thought was so easy, the next found tiring. They felt that pumping water by hand was a hardship and took so long. So up went a windmill. Ah, the whole family was amazed at the utter convenience of it all. No more standing, puffing, and pumping. All they had to do was walk to the well and dip the water from a large wooden tank. It seemed so much easier that this generation never imagined the next might balk at the trip to the well. But that is exactly what happened.

What? Walk to the well and carry all that water! I guess not. So in goes a system of water pipes. Ah, what grand luxury. Water pumped right into the house, water waiting and ready twenty-four hours of the day at the turn of a spigot. Turn it open, and there's water to wash the face, water to cook a meal, water to fill the teakettle.

Fill the teakettle, did you say? What for? To heat water to wash the dishes? Ha, guess again. That's not for us. We're the next generation. Who has time to heat water when we want it? Why, with the water heater installed, all we need to do is turn the tap, and there is all the hot water we like.

That brings us up to the present. What will the next generation want? We immediately think, "But hot water on the tap, that's so handy to wash dishes with, we can't imagine that our children won't be satisfied with that."

No, of course not. Our parents couldn't imagine that we wouldn't be satisfied with *their* luxuries, either. What we appreciate, our children take for granted.

Satan likes to make us believe that if we only had this or that, we could be so much happier. If only the church would allow this, we'd be satisfied. We wouldn't ask for more. We'd be content.

Would it really work that way? Let's look around with our eyes open. If having an abundance of material things would bring contentment, then those who have the most should be the most contented. Who has more material things than the people of the world? Anything they like, they can go and buy. New cars.

Fancy clothes. Vacations to faraway places. Anything. You name it, and the world has it. And if they don't, they invent it.

Are they contented? Are they satisfied with what they have? The answer is obvious. One look at the headlines of a newspaper should convince anyone. Riots. Strikes. Demands. Boycotts. Protests. Marches. Welfare. Unrest. Crime. Divorces. Suicides. Rebellions. Violence. Tension.

There never was a generation that had so much and appreciated it so little. Young people grow up and never raise a finger to work. Still they are dissatisfied and run away by the thousands. No, the people of the world aren't content with all the luxuries they have. Jesus said long ago, "A man's life does not consist in the abundance of the things he possesses" (Luke 12:15).

The time has come for each of us to stop and ask some questions. Where are we as Plain people? Where have we come from? Where are we going? What factors have brought us to where we are today? In what ways have we suffered from too much materialism? To what degree do we have the same spirit the world has, the spirit of always wanting more?

What are the solutions? Perhaps the first step is to become aware of how good we really have it, and to realize what spoiled children we have become.

Another thing that would help would be to renew our convictions on the teachings of the Bible showing the importance of simple living. We need to rediscover that a simple way of life, separated and apart from the world, is indeed God's pattern for his people.

However scriptural simple living is, it is not an automatic passport to heaven. Thousands of people live simple lives, with just a roof above their heads and a dirt floor beneath their feet, and so few earthly possessions that they can load them all onto an oxcart. They may still live ungodly lives, wallowing in sin and poverty. Hand in hand with our simple living must be a devout faith in God, honesty of conviction, and an earnest desire for the brotherhood. Olden times were more simple, but that doesn't mean that everything that is old is good. Our goal is not to pattern after the early Americans, but after the early Christians.

Will the same trends and influences that have wrecked families and communities in the world around us also destroy us in time? If we follow the same route, travel in the same train, we cannot expect to arrive at a different destination. Trailing fifty years behind the world isn't going to get us where we want to be. Those who ride in the caboose are going to the same place as the engineer.

There is constant pressure in the surrounding society to conform in such areas as travel and work. Yet there is plenty of evidence, if we care to see it, that such things as tractor farming and automobile travel are deadly in the long run, eroding the values of brotherhood, simple living, family sharing, and meaningful community relationship. If we allow ourselves to become like spoiled children, always wanting more and more, we cannot expect long to resist the temptation these and other modern inventions present to us and our children. If our love of ease becomes greater than our willingness to deny ourselves and to sacrifice, we are well down the road of no return, the one-way street of modernism and materialism.

We don't need more conveniences as much as we need more convictions. In this world of emphasis on luxury and earthly possessions, it may be difficult to be content with little. But it is impossible to be content with much.

—E. Stoll

FOUR

Marriage and Family

PERHAPS NOTHING IS MORE VITAL to the Amish way of life than the family and community. The very title *Family Life* points to its importance. Yet this is also an arena with many challenges, especially since the Amish do not accept divorce. We often hear the promise "till death do us part." For the Amish, it is indeed a promise. But married life is not always wedded bliss, whether we are Amish or not.

In the relationship of husband and wife, the Amish find parallels to those between God and the church. In the family, matters of faith and their application must be played out in practical, everyday terms. Here religion and reality come together in the Amish community, for better or for worse.

Marriage, a Most Sacred Institution

There are three reasons why a wedding is one of the most unique of the services held by our churches today. For one thing, it is the most joyous. The second reason is that a wedding is such a serious event, where a lifetime commitment is being made.

The third reason is that it is such a sacred event because it is an *Abbildung*, a representation of the spiritual union between Christ and his bride, the church.

In Lancaster County (Pa.), it is customary for the Amish wedding season to begin after the fall communion and continue until Christmas. The young married couples then spend the rest of the winter in visiting. Uncles and aunts receive an overnight visit. It is the couple's way of starting out on the journey of life together.

I am thankful that in our churches, marriage vows are taken very seriously and are considered a lifetime commitment. If we listen carefully to the words of the marriage ceremony and to the vows exchanged, we find it inconceivable that any provision can be made for divorce and remarriage. I do not believe our churches could have survived and maintained their separation from the world over the centuries if we had not taken the marriage vows so seriously and literally.

We believe reconciliation is the key word to solving marital problems. As long as remarriage remains an option, reconciliation does not get a fair trial. Reconciliation works satisfactorily only when the scriptural requirement is enforced as the only option the church has to offer: possible separation but no remarriage.

—D. Wagler

Making Marriage a Success

We must think of marriage as being more than a civil contract. It constitutes a bond that only God can bind. Two souls are united into one, to live together as one. The apostle Paul says, "So ought men to love their wives as their own bodies. He that loveth his wife loveth himself" [Ephesians 5:28].

The happiness of the husband and wife determines the kind of home the children will be born into.

No one is born a good marriage partner. [Each spouse] must pay the price of being one. The happiest marriages are those in which people do what they can to make each other happy, instead of using each other to make themselves happy. Marriage partners must remember that everyone has faults and needs forgiveness. Therefore, it takes the force of true love to blend two different personalities into one happy union. Love, if it is to grow, must be nurtured. It must not be taken for granted, even after marriage.

Many homes are unhappy because the husbands do not function as partners with their wives. They are quick to quote the Bible verse that says, "Wives, submit yourselves unto your own husbands," or "The husband is the head of the wife" [Ephesians 5:22-23]. Wives do not become servants, slaves, or puppets.

Woman was not taken from man's head for him to lord over her. She was not taken from his feet so that he could trample on her or kick her around. But she was taken from his side, close to his heart, thus being a loving partner to help him with life's responsibilities [Genesis 2:18-23]. Among [her duties] are allowing the husband to be the head of the house, converting a house into a home, and assuming the responsibilities of motherhood. Certainly the submission of the wife does not mean slavish subjection, but a joyful working together for a common cause.

—Anonymous

Heirs Together

Some husbands get the idea that their position of authority in the home gives them the right to be harsh, demanding, and unreasonable. The answer to this problem is *love*. The apostle Paul writes in Ephesians 5:25, "Husbands, love your wives, even as Christ also loved the church, and gave himself for it." That is a big commandment, for Christ loved the church so much that he was willing to die for it.

It is true that the Bible puts a lot of emphasis on how wives should obey, should submit, should be humble and faithful. Too often men forget that the Bible also says some things about the duty of husbands. More is required of husbands than of wives. It is hard to submit to authority in the right spirit, but it is even harder to use that authority in the right way. To be trusted with a position of authority is not something to be taken lightly. It is not an easy place to fill. Let us remember that those who misuse the authority entrusted to them will someday have to give an account for their actions just as well as those who are placed under authority and refuse to submit to it.

—E. Stoll

The Place of Women
Distinct Roles

It's not a question at all of whether or not women are as good as men. The Bible teaches us clearly that men and women are equal. But being equal in worth does not mean being the same in calling. This is where modern women make their greatest mistake. Men are still men, women still women, no matter how equal. Each has been assigned separate and distinct roles by the great Creator.

If marriage were to be fifty-fifty, that would result in two people being the head of the home. Not only is that not scriptural, it isn't even workable. As one writer summed it up, "In any kind of relationship involving more than one person, there must be the head of the relationship. Further, no organization, large or small, commercial or philanthropic, secular or religious, has more than one president, ruler, or head."

—E. Stoll

Subordinate but Not Inferior

Subordinate does not mean inferior. God has set up authority everywhere, such as in government, the church, the school, and the home. The citizens shall be subordinate to the government, but this does not make them inferior. Lay members shall be subordinate to the leaders of the church, but this does not make inferior people out of them [Hebrews 13:17]. Even the most brilliant pupil should be subordinate to his teacher, but this does not make him inferior. The same thing applies in the home between children and their parents, and between man and wife.

—Staff

Mutual Encouragement in Marriage

A husband wrote to ask what others do when the wife gets a crying spell. "Do you comfort her lovingly, or just ignore it all and hope she will get over it again?" Here are two answers:

Meeting Each Other's Needs

Since the husband cared enough to write for advice about his wife's tears, I want to say, "God bless him. Talk to your wife! Work toward an honest, open relationship." My husband loved me but couldn't handle his emotions. If I cried, he would yell at the children or start a tirade of how inconsiderate they were to me. Most of the time all I needed was a strong shoulder to lean on, or a sympathetic ear.

Don't condemn. Wives pretty well know their shortcomings. Working at home alone gives one time to think. We need to know that we are not alone, that we can't be expected to be a tower of strength every moment of our lives. Be her protector, her comforter, her friend. You can be sure that if you understand each other's needs, she can be these things to you also!

—Anonymous

In Favor of Sharing Problems

In the most common situations, the husbands of the weeping women have about as many fears and as much lack of confidence as their wives. I guess to really prove my sympathy to my wife, I should share my feelings and weep with her. But I try to keep my balance and avoid extreme feelings. I know from experience how completely weak and drained a body can become with the habit of being afraid of the future or others, and of myself.

The most important thing is for the wife to talk to her husband about her fears when the load gets too heavy. Being afraid to talk about our fears is more than anybody can live with for too long.

My guess is that if all the men who have gone into the silo and cried alone would write to *Family Life*, we would also have many letters.

—Anonymous

The Long Divorce

For the past several months, Lester and the rest of Valentine Zook's carpenter crew had been working on a new house for Dick Waffles and his wife, Pam. When they arrived at the house they were building, Lester saw at once that something strange was going on. Valentine called Lester and the others over to him. His face was solemn.

"You probably noticed that Dick was here," he began bluntly. "He was pretty upset, and I guess he had reason to be. Pam left him last night, and she plans to file for divorce. Dick doesn't want to spend any more money on this house, so he wants us to finish up a few things we started, and then he'll put the house up for sale as it is."

Married one day, divorced the next. Lester kept shaking his head. "I wonder how it would feel to wake up one morning and be told your wife is leaving you, is going to file for a divorce," Lester said to himself. He turned to John. "I just can't get over this."

John shook his head. "It does seem sudden to us, I guess," he said. "But don't let that deceive you."

Lester felt sick at heart. "I took my frustrations out on Lavina and was too proud to apologize and admit how unreasonable I had been." He had hurt his wife for hardly any reason at all, just because the baby cried and farm prices kept going out of sight.

[As they worked, John shared his thinking.] "There's no way a man and wife who have a good relationship today are going to get a divorce tomorrow. People just can't do that when love and affection is there. I'm afraid Dick and Pam were divorced for a long time—not on the outside, not legally, not according to the law. Of course not. But on the inside they've been divorced for a long time. They must have been. The inside divorce always comes first.

"Our people don't believe in divorce and that is good, as far as it goes. But I'm afraid we have some divorces among us and don't know it. Husbands and wives still live in the same house, but that is about all. Their love for each other is missing. They don't feel close or loyal to each other. On the outside they are married. On the inside they are divorced. They argue. They disagree. They work against each other. [For this separation to happen,] there must have been a long time of misunderstanding, of quarreling with each other, of not apologizing, of refusing to bend to each other."

Three o'clock in the afternoon found the work completed on the Waffles' house. "Would you mind stopping in town a bit on the way home?" Lester asked John. "My wife needs a stand for the bedroom. She said she'd do without, and we'd save the money and put it toward buying a farm. I just decided today that I'd surprise her and make a neat little bed stand for her."

They poked the boards into the back of the buggy box. Then Lester said, "We're all set, I guess, except for a few items I need at the grocery store." He went straight to the freezer. For himself, he'd rather have butterscotch ripple or just plain vanilla, but he knew that his wife's favorite ice cream was maple walnut.

John's horse stood patiently while Lester unloaded the boards and bag of groceries beside their small house. As soon as John drove away, Lester opened the door and ran into the house. Lavina was at the sink, stirring something in a large mixing bowl.

"Are you baking something?" he asked. But then he knew the answer. He saw it in her face and all over the kitchen sink. She was planning to bake a carrot cake, a cake she didn't really care for, but which was his favorite. She was doing it as a special favor for him.

All of a sudden, his throat felt tight and funny, but he struggled to control himself. He took her by the arm, led her silently to the window, and pointed out at the things he had brought home from town.

"You remembered!" she said, her face lighting up.

"There's everything I need to finish it tonight, I hope, even if I have to work late. But most of all, I wanted to say I'm sorry."

She didn't let him say more. Sure enough, she was crying again. Only this time he was crying right along with her, and he wasn't even ashamed of the tears, only sorry that he had waited so long.

—Anonymous

Maturity in Marriage

Before we were married, we discovered we both loved pizza, so we decided we had a lot in common. (Of course, we didn't base our marriage on that.) Now, after fourteen years and six children, there have been times I have wondered, "Do we have *anything* in common besides that?" But in my more sane moments, I know we do. First, we love each other.

How I tried to reform my husband, the poor soul! He likes to get up late in the morning, start the day slowly, then commence to be really on the ball around eleven, sometimes not until after dinner [lunch]. By then, he may have decided which of his numerous jobs he will work on that day. Some of the jobs have been started for days, some for weeks, some for years. He is never excited or upset. He takes everything as it comes. He has no concept of time. He is very forgetful, and sometimes is sure it's Tuesday when it's really Friday. He loves to go anywhere, day or night. And oh, he loves popcorn.

Now the extreme opposite—*me*. I get out of bed with a hop and a skip, the earlier the better, ready to tackle the job I have already planned the night before. I work at it diligently until it is finished. I work full speed all morning and into the afternoon. Then toward suppertime, I start slowing down, and by eight in the evening, I'm ready for bed. I'm prone to outbursts of alarm, distress, or even anger. I continually watch the clock; everything must be on time. I despise being late, especially to church, which I enjoy going to. Otherwise, I am happy to stay at home. And I dread popcorn.

By now you're [probably] wondering how we can stand each other. It took a while, but one thing we have always been able to do is talk things over. That's one of the keys—communication. I remember well the time he asked me, "How would you like to be like I am?"

"Impossible," I answered.

Then he explained to me that this was what I was trying to do to him, trying to make him the way I am, and he said that's impossible too. I began to realize we can complement each other. In many areas, we compromise. It is essential to give in to each other, but it is not necessary to lose one's individual identity.

Even if we are extremely opposite, we seem to have exactly what the other needs to make a well-rounded union of two personalities combined in one.

However, the very thing that gives us this understanding of each other, the very vital part of our marriage, is praying together. Come what may, we have an anchor for our souls. Even if there are stormy times, we know we have a sure foundation. I don't even begrudge him his popcorn once a week. But please, not *every* day.

—Anonymous

Question from a Young Mother

We are a young couple with our first, perfectly normal baby boy. Since his arrival, I feel very much deprived of the freedom I used to have, since I now am tied down to all that goes into caring for a baby. Because of this, I feel I don't love our baby the way God meant for us to love children.

I feel guilty while caring for him because of the resentment I at times feel. I would not want to give him up, but my own selfishness still bothers me.

Can I help my husband raise our baby in a God-fearing way without God's contentment in my heart? Have other mothers had such feelings? If so, did you overcome them, and how?

—*Tied-down Young Mother*

Response 1

Mothering is an art and a growing experience. Some young mothers seem to sail into motherhood without any problems, while others need time to grow into it. But remember, you can never be a perfect mother, nor can you have a perfect baby, so don't expect too much.

It is natural to sometimes resent the tiny baby, especially one who is fussy. Unless you feel a constant resentment, I think you should accept your feelings and realize that they will pass.

Truly, loving your baby will take time, just as loving your husband came gradually. I feel sure you can help your husband raise your little one in God's way. Someday soon your little one will give you a hug and a kiss and say, "I love you." Then you will feel amply repaid for motherhood.

—E. R.

Response 2

You say you are deprived of your freedom you had. Freedom for what? Freedom to help others in your spare time, do errands, or visit the sick and elderly? Or freedom to go to Tupperware and Stanley parties, or garage sales, to read books, or to go to the neighbor's place on evenings to play games?

Yes, perhaps one would have a little battle with tied-down feelings. But perhaps if you had empty arms for several years, aching to hold your own child, or had doctor bills to pay just because of trying to discover why your longed-for children are not on the way—you would be glad for tied-down feelings.

Perhaps, of course, I do not know how you feel, for we are . . .

—*Childless*

Acceptance Is the Answer

I don't feel God chose us couples to be childless because we're unworthy. Why don't we meet this childless state as a challenge from God to see what we make of it? Are we going to waste our time being bitter and filled with self-pity? Sometimes I wonder if we childless couples' biggest problem might be hurt pride. Do we feel odd or like outcasts because we can't have what most couples have? If we can't be happy without children, what makes us think we'd be happy with them? If we can't meet the challenge of *not* having children, what makes us think we'd be capable of meeting the challenge of having children?

—Anonymous

Are the Children His or Hers?

Our family is four-fifths male. The boys are "mine" when there are diapers to change, heads to wash, clothes to mend, Band-Aids to put on, clothes to wash, cookies to make, apples to peel, and small quarrels to stop.

The boys are "his" when there are baths to take, hair to cut, trips to make to the feed or parts store, toys to fix, a new calf is being born, enough snow for toboggan rides down the steepest hills, and extra-firm discipline is needed.

They are "ours" when we have family devotion, go for walks or wade in the stream, attend church, or visit Grandpa's; when they get sick at night or enter school life; when we do farm chores; and when we sit around the table for a meal.

—Anonymous

An Indiana Grandma Remembers

I am now a grandmother, with not so many chores and no little children to take care of. We raised nine children, and nearly all of them are married. When they were small, we would get up at four thirty or five. This gave us time to chore together, have breakfast, and have a little work done before the little ones were up. If they were awake when we came in, Daddy would lend a helping hand while I got breakfast. After breakfast, all who could toddle would go out with him until he was ready to go to the field. Then they would come in or play in the yard. As the noon hour neared, I would fill the horses' mangers with hay and dole out oats for them.

When Daddy came in for dinner, the children all came in with him. He would see to it that each one was washed and at the right place around the table. Sometimes one would not want to eat this or that or was naughty. They would go to the porch. All the other children would not say a word, but would sympathize with the one on the porch. When Daddy and the child came in, the eats tasted good. But this did not have to happen often.

After dinner, Daddy would take the little ones under school age for a nap. Toward evening, at four or four thirty, I would quit my work and start choring. We worked together. Often after supper, they all went out to play in the yard. A lot of times I would think that Daddy would have many other things to do instead of playing with them. I always worked. Now I can see where he was a better daddy than I was a mother. They remember and treasure this more than anything else he could have done for them.

—Anonymous

The Family That Plays Together

Children are born with imagination, and all they need is a chance to develop it. A rag doll is just as good as an expensive wind-up beauty.

The imagination of children can soon give dolls the ability to cry, drink, sleep, and wet themselves. Yet most parents find it easier to buy a box of "performing" toys than to take time to help their children with something that requires their presence and interest, plus imagination. So in choosing a game for children, look for something they can do things with, rather than something that will do things for them. A half dozen chairs lined up behind each other will create an instant train that children can ride to all sorts of places. Such a train can "chug chug chug," whistle at the crossings, load and unload passengers. The battery never runs down, though after half an hour the parents may wish it did!

Beware lest you spoil the child's natural knack for imaginative play. Two of my brother's boys were playing in our yard. We had an old discarded lawnmower without the cutting blade. They had this lawnmower, and one was hitched to the front, pulling it with a twine string, while the other grasped the handle. No grass was cut. I felt a bit of pity for them that they had to keep imagining they were cutting the lawn.

"You got the lawn mowed?" I asked them after a while.

They stopped and looked at me in surprise, amazed at my adult ignorance. "Why, no," said the younger of the two, "we're not mowing anything. We're plowing this field!"

Properly put into my place, I retreated, realizing that I still had a few things to learn before I would be worthy of helping children play.

—E. Stoll

Not Mine, but Ours

Somehow the family should be such a close-knit unit that sharing is the most natural thing in the world. Sharing cannot be difficult where there is a strong feeling of love and appreciation for each other. Learning to share our toys and childhood belongings should be the foundation for easy sharing on a wider scale in the adult world. However, families are not only for sharing material possessions.

More important yet is the sharing of feelings, of problems, and of joys. In the shelter of the home, we should be able to discuss with frankness our hopes and disappointments, knowing that we are speaking to those we can trust.

Another thing that should be shared within the family is work. No home is without work, and it is fortunate that this is so. Any child who doesn't grow up helping with dishes, or doing chores, or running errands has been cheated out of a good start in life. The family should be the place to learn to work cheerfully and well, even eagerly. Work should be shared by everyone willingly chipping in, and not by a legalistic insistence that each does an earmarked portion.

A happy family life requires giving of ourselves. We must learn to sacrifice, learn to give up our will for the other.

Some families are just so many individuals with the same last name, living in the same house. They seem to lead separate lives, go their own ways, each independent of the other. If you ask where another member of the family is, they rarely know. Apparently, they don't know where the rest of the family is, or what they are doing. Each is busy living their own life. They lack the essential elements of a joyful family life—love, togetherness, loyalty, sharing.

These sad little groups of lonely individuals are not families at all. They are failures. They are missing out on one of the greatest challenges on this earth—building a meaningful family relationship where work, possessions, and even feelings can be shared in love and trust.

—E. Stoll

FIVE

The Young

EVERY SOCIETY RECOGNIZES ITS YOUNG as its future. The family and school are integral in producing a "successful citizen." In the Amish community, where private one-room schooling is the norm, parents are involved in the lives and education of their children throughout the eight grades. They also know that not all the skills and lessons for life are learned sitting behind a desk.

The Amish, like parents everywhere, have their successes and failures when it comes to rearing children. They, too, worry about being too strict on the one hand, or too liberal on the other. Like most parents, their emotions can sometimes get in the way of making the best decisions for their children, and they suffer great pain when a child goes "astray." These writings are some of the most touching and compelling to be found in the pages of *Family Life*.

Children Are Treasures

Menno Simons made a statement on the way parents should feel about their children that is so strong that most of us today would hesitate to express it so forcefully: "This is the chief and principal care of the saints, that their children may fear God, do right, and be saved."

Perhaps herein lies the greatest single difference between the teaching of the Plain churches and that of the more liberal churches—the degree of emphasis on child training. This concern for [bringing up and educating] our children is best summed up by the German word *Kinderzucht*, not matched exactly by any English word.

With the loss of *Kinderzucht*, many other things get lost rapidly from our families and churches. Our very lives center on our families and our children. They are our future church, our most treasured possession. This is in direct contrast to the world around us, where children are in the way, especially in large families—meaning any family with more than two children, in today's society. Worldly parents often find children getting on their nerves and under their feet. They want longer and longer school terms so the children will be out of the way. When the children are at home, the TV set is often used as a babysitter.

In our way of life, however, children are useful, needed, and wanted. They help with the work around the farm and do household chores, learning to be useful at a young age. Instead of sighing with relief when the school term begins in the fall and groaning when it lets out in the spring, Amish parents react in reverse.

Probably no theme comes up in our sermons more frequently than the great responsibility that parents have to bring up their children in "the fear of the Lord." We have all heard again and again the saying that "children are the only treasures on earth we can take with us to heaven."

—E. Stoll

Concerned about Schools

The greatest threat against our schools does not come from the outside but from the inside. If we are careless and unconcerned about who is teaching our children and what they are teaching them, then our schools will soon reach the point of no return. If we do not realize the need for our *own* schools and the dangers of sending our children to public schools, then unfavorable rulings from the courts cannot do us any real harm. They can make us suffer for our convictions. But the faith that's not worth suffering for is not worth living for.

—Anonymous

Parental Responsibility

Government officials would like us to believe it is their right to give our children secular education. This is false. The Bible teaches that it is the parents' duty to provide or oversee all their children's training, religious or secular.

Can you control what is taught to your children in the public schools? Can you see to it that their teachers will not be atheists, evolutionists, immoral, or unqualified in some other way? Very unlikely. In a private school, we can control what is taught and by whom.

The government not only tolerates us in exercising this privilege, but also grudgingly admits it is our right. I know it costs us more, but to what better use could we put our money? I know there is also risk of a private school getting out of control, but the public school is already far out of control. It teaches our children gross untruths about our origin and the creation. It also exposes them to all kinds of vice and sin. With proper direction and control, we can safely operate private schools.

—Anonymous

A Waste?

"Mr. Troyer," said a public schoolteacher a few years ago to an Amish father, "do you realize that your son, Bennie, has an exceptional mind? He always gets straight As without even working. You should certainly see that he goes to high school and college. It would be a shame, a terrible waste, if he didn't."

The Amish father shook his head. The schoolteacher shook his, too, although for a different reason. He went home muttering to himself, "A terrible waste. All that talent, and all he'll ever amount to is an old-fashioned farmer, sweating in the field, tilling the soil with his hands like a common peasant, when he might be a doctor or a dentist. Who knows, maybe even an artist or a poet."

A waste? Yes, Bennie might get on in the world. He might well reach fame, wealth, and pleasure. But what if he lost his soul? Would that not be the greatest waste of all?

—Anonymous

Special Education

Several years ago here in Lancaster County we started a "special education school" for nervous, hyperactive, and slow learners, or any other children who couldn't cope in regular school. Classes are held in the basement of a regular [one-room] school. Thus these children have recess at the same time and can play with the other children.

The two teachers have about sixteen pupils. They need to have much patience with their pupils, but the results are surprising. Children who would have little chance in a regular school learn arithmetic and learn to read and understand what they read. Evidently, outsiders felt we would not be qualified to operate such a class. It did look like a big mountain to the board that was elected to get it started.

Though I am not closely associated with the class, I can still say that the results appear to be very good. For some of these children, I believe it is like filling a bottle that has a small neck. It is possible to fill such a bottle, but it takes much time and patience. For children who otherwise would not learn, it opens a new world to be able to count and read, even if it's only some of the simplest books.

—D. F.

What Troubled Linda

Linda was discouraged with teaching. It almost seemed to her that it was pointless to have parochial schools. What was the use of going to all that effort and expense to shield the children from harmful companions if later they associated freely with young people who seemed to undo all the good accomplished in school?

Surely it is good and right that we have our own schools. We seek to teach and train children in what is upbuilding, and to shield them from the harmful company and environment of public schools. But it is too bad if we are not concerned in providing an equally upbuilding environment later, among the young people. Are we concerned only about our little children and not about our big children?

It seems that the greatest reason why more is not being done about this problem is simply that we don't care enough. If we really cared, would we or could we casually visit together about our crops and neighbors all Sunday afternoon? Meanwhile, in the room upstairs, our young people are keeping the air blue with smoke and playing cards and entertaining each other with off-color jokes. Would we as parents, if we really cared as we should, go ahead week after week, washing and ironing clothes for our young people, which they wear in disobedience to the church?

If we really cared, would we let our young people go away in the evening without knowing where they are going, or what they will be doing, or with whom they will be spending their time? Would we go to bed on Saturday evening with our daughters upstairs and the house unlocked so boys can enter and leave at will? This is a setup so evil that it is shameful to mention. One can hardly imagine parents so unconcerned as to tolerate it.

It is time we looked around and asked what kind of teachers our children have when they reach their teenage years. A teacher is anyone we learn from. Who will our children learn from more readily than the friends and companions they are with?

—E. Stoll

Generation Gap

One of the basic rules of life is that it takes time to build strong emotional ties. For strong ties of friendship to develop, people need to spend a certain amount of time together.

No doubt our children spend more time in the company of their peers than any other generation before them. Our people have certainly been right to resist consistently any government demands to send our children to high school. It is already bad enough that they are away from their parents for eight school terms. Perhaps we have already gone along too far with today's educational system.

Three hundred years ago, children were at home with the family during all their growing years. We would not want to go back to that. In those days, few could read. At the same time, we should be aware of the danger in children being away from their parents too much, and in the company of their peers. We have our own schools, and that is good. This is our way of guarding against bad company for our children. But perhaps it is time for us to see that even good company, if it detracts from the ties between parent and child, can also be a harmful thing.

This same thing is true beyond the level of school years. Yet even many of the most well-meaning parents see no danger in young people being together too much. In fact, some parents call for *more youth activity* as a solution to the problems of our young people.

There is a motto that "the family that prays together, stays together." That says a lot in a few words, but it doesn't say enough. It is surely an oversimplification. A family needs to do more than pray together. It needs to work together, visit friends together, read together, plan things together, eat together, share their joy and sorrows, hopes and disappointments. In short, the family needs to *live together*.

It is true that young people need something to do. But parents should look harder for things [young people] can do with the family that will serve to strengthen the ties between children and parents, rather than between children and their peers.

—Staff

Earning Money

Responses to a question on how parents handle money their children have earned:

When the opportunity came to earn money outside the home, my parents let us have half and invested [it] in savings accounts. With our own children, because we have a large family with physical handicaps and large family responsibilities, our children had to take adult responsibilities at a young age. Therefore, we started giving them an allowance for being on time or doing their chores well. We then allowed them to spend half their earnings under our supervision, also teaching them to remember the poor.

—*A Father*

It's the child's duty to work for his parents until of age, though a small weekly allowance might be all right. I think it's fine for the child to establish a savings account, but no checking account. The father should keep the bank book till the child is of age. I know of parents who allow their children a certain percent of their paychecks (money earned away from home—10, 15, 20 percent, or whatever the parents decide) to invest in savings. When the children are twenty-one, with the accumulated interest, what a surprise they will have.

—A. W.

In some homes, when children reach sixteen years of age, they are allowed to keep half their earnings till twenty-one. I feel it fair for children to keep all their wages at eighteen and be encouraged to save it for starting housekeeping or farming.

—A. H.

I am satisfied with the way my parents taught me to handle money.

I went through four stages:

- Penny bank: I had a yellow piggy bank, where all my money went, whether from gifts or from rewards for doing special jobs.

- Savings account: When I had accumulated enough money, my piggy bank was emptied. Dad sawed it open, helped me count it, and took it to the bank. Before I was of age, I couldn't withdraw any money without his signature.

- Ten percent: When I was old enough to hold a paying job, I was allowed to keep 10 percent of what I earned.

- Checking account: Dad knew I'd need a checking account once I handled my own expenses and went on my own. He introduced me to checking, and my savings account remained untouched. What I earned went into the checking account.

Thus I was taught to save before I was taught how to spend.
—Laura Z. Martin

Hired Girls

Today was our communion service. It was a peaceful day outside, as peaceful as the hearts of those inside who partook of the Lord's Supper. The minister's words were inspiring and a blessing to all listening ears. I kept looking at the stern expressions of these folks in our small community. A few silent tears escaped my eyes, and I felt a heavy heart.

My heartache was made worse two weeks ago when I was punished at counsel meeting, but it didn't start there. It didn't even start two years ago. In fact, it goes back much further.

In our family, I was second in line. My parents never had a lot, but we never went to bed hungry, or wore patched clothes to church. They tried to teach me right from wrong, and I'm thankful to God for my Amish heritage.

I started working out at an early age. My first job for non-Amish people was at the tender, vulnerable age of thirteen. My parents didn't realize the years of heartache I would live through by letting me have a better paying job. I have an outgoing personality, which makes it easier for me to accept different people. I had little or no problems adjusting.

For two solid years, I was gone from Monday morning until Friday night. I had every convenience imaginable. In no time, I could control every switch and knew how to push every button. Of course, I had free evenings, and I soon had my favorite TV shows. I could recognize a radio station by hearing the DJ's voice. I learned most of the songs and often sang along. I read newspapers and books of all kinds. I adapted to their views and ideas. Without realizing it, I was living two different lives.

Now I'm twenty-eight, and I realize my many years working out have been somewhat of an exception. I've been employed by the families of an air force pilot, a police officer, doctors, and even a professional football player, plus other more common people. I've been acquainted with just as many different religions and attended church at least once with most of them. I've had opportunities and encouragement to go into nursing, dental assistance, secretarial, and other types of work from all the well-meaning people who always told me I had too much intelligence to waste on housecleaning or babysitting. I began joining church at sixteen and was baptized at seventeen.

I really have tried to live up to the rules and regulations of the communities I've lived in. Despite this, there [seemed to be many] times when I was making confessions in church for misdeeds. Now I'm beginning to see or understand that no one is doing anything to be cruel. But for the church to be pure, it must remove any leaven of evil [1 Corinthians 5].

I am the one who must change, but after all this time, it seems impossible. How can I change the inside of me to be the Amish person I should be? How can I undo the influence of all those years?

I pray to be like the girl down the road who gets up at five o'clock in the morning and milks seven or eight cows, and who doesn't have to be away from home day after day after day. I only hope more parents realize the dangers in letting their young girls go out, away from home and under the influence of the world. Believe me, it's not worth the money.

All I can say is that it's a miracle I'm still Amish. I'm not sure I can stay in my beloved community. The Lord knows I want to stay, but my best may not be good enough. I'm at the crossroads of my life, and I don't know which way to turn. The scars will always be with me. I'll suffer the effects for the rest of my life.

If my letter can help just one parent realize the danger in working out, if I can save just one girl from all the heartache I've been through, this letter will have been well worth my time.

—M. B.

Courtship and Wild Oats

The Right Time for Courtship

It is hard to look around the Plain churches today and not get the feeling that we have far too much courtship *before* marriage, and not nearly enough *after* marriage. Young people who make every effort to win each other's love before marriage often do not put forth much effort after marriage.

Young men will travel miles before the wedding day to show how devoted they are to their special one. Ten years later, they find it too much of a task to get up from the table to help her with the dishes. Boys who stayed up all night with their date refuse to take their turn to wrestle with a sick baby at midnight.

Ah, if only we could get a little more courtship into marriage, how much happier would be many of our homes.

Marriage, to be worthwhile, requires intelligent thought and continued effort. Good marriages do not just happen. They do not result from having married the "right" one as much as from the blessings of God, persistent work, and loving labor to make ourselves the "right" one.

—Staff

Our Inexcusable Silence

Sometimes ignoring something is the best solution. But many times it is not. One problem too many of our Plain churches have been ignoring for generations is unclean talk and low courtship and moral standards of their young people. I can think of no other problem in our churches about which so many people are silent. Parents ignore it. Whole communities of ministers and bishops ignore it. But there is no longer any hope that if we just pretend the problem isn't there, maybe it will go away.

It has been getting worse for generations. Yet there is a terrible disease, a spiritual plague spreading in too many of our communities. There are even some communities where there is hardly any shame or disgrace anymore for couples to come to marriage with purity gone. That is a terrible foundation upon which to build a Christian home. (Thankfully, there are also many communities where such conditions are unheard of.)

If we ignore low courtship standards and pretend they aren't there, the day will surely come when we will have to answer for not only the shameful problem itself, but also our inexcusable silence about it.

—E. Stoll

So-Called Amish

I was both shocked and surprised one day last week when our neighbor boy came over and said, "My friends and I really saw something last evening."

When I asked him what it was, he said they had stopped at a gas station up along Route 23. A car pulled in with three Amish boys and three Amish girls in it. He said the boys were dressed in "loud" clothes, and the girls jumped out and ran for the restrooms. They were soon back with their hair hanging down to their shoulders and dressed in skirts which he said were "real short."

They drove off down the road. These boys were curious to know where these so-called Amish young folks were going. They followed them up the road and saw them pull in at the fire hall, where a dance was being held. There they were laughing and talking among the worldly people.

I just had to wonder, Where were these young folks' parents? It seems to me these young people should have been at home that evening. Things like this hurt me very much when I hear them. I believe that surely the Lord must also be grieved.

—Anonymous

Taking Responsibility

Young people sow their wild oats, living undisciplined and lustful lives until they want to get married. Then all of a sudden, they decide to join the church. Many people suspect deep down inside that they are joining the church to get married, and not because they have repented of their sins. Yet parents and ministers go along with this mockery, remarking to one another how thankful they are that the young people still have a desire to join the church. Sure enough, they are barely baptized until they get published [have their engagement announced in church] and married.

What is important is that for too long, too many of us have been taking the wrong attitude. We have been excusing ourselves with the lie "One man can do nothing." Why don't we all make up our minds to do what we can, however little that may be? We might be surprised over the years what the total may add up to.

—E. Stoll

Cars

The Faded Flag

A visitor once related how he was visiting relatives in another community. He noticed that many of the Amish homes had a car parked in the driveway. In the course of his visit, he had the chance to ask one of the ministers in that district about this.

"Yes," the minister explained, "we feel parents should allow their son to live at home with his car if he has one. That way the parents can still talk to the son, and explain to him how wrong it is for him to have his worldly life. The parents don't ride with the son, of course." The visitor was somewhat satisfied. That evening, he happened to be a supper guest in a home where a son was at home with his car. All evening the son was laughing and talking with his young brothers and sisters about radio songs and sports events. Worse yet, when the visitor was ready to go to another place for the night, instead of the parents hitching up and taking him over, they said, "Our son will drive you over with his car. You don't mind, do you? The church doesn't want us to ride with him, but it won't hurt if you do."

The visitor was stunned. Was this how the parents admonished their son for his wrongdoing, by asking him to transport visitors with his car? What message were the parents giving their son? They would have claimed that they were waving a red flag to their son. But who could blame the son for thinking the flag looked more like a white one that told him to proceed, the way was clear?

—E. Stoll

To the Boy Who'd Like a Car

How will a car help you? To get a date with a girl who said she won't go with you in a buggy? Do you realize what kind of wife she would make? She would never be content until she had the very best (or is it the worst?). You might never be able to afford a home the way she would want it, so she'd always be complaining and dissatisfied.

You say you want it so you can be away from home. You can go across the world and back again and never find a home like the one you left. Where would you find people who care what you do, provide all your meals for nothing, keep your room cleaned and your closet filled with clothes?

Tired of your chores! Would you rather get up in a messy apartment, hunt for something clean to wear, and wish for a breakfast like Mom's, but instead end up eating some cold cereal?

You want to prove Dad and Mom can't keep you from getting a car if you want to? No, maybe they can't. But neither can they keep you from going to a fire that burns forever.

You may think that as long as your parents keep praying for you, you'll be all right. Don't forget, you'll have to make your own wrongs right. You can't expect your parents to make it right for you if you get killed in an auto crash.

Are you just planning on having your car a couple of years? Remember, a car will take you further and further from home. What if you get so involved that you can't come back to your home? If you do come back, marry, and have a pleasant home, what will you tell your children when they want a car too?

—A Girl with an Aching Heart

Leaving the Community
Are You Really Going?

Tomorrow is the day, the parting of the ways, and you must make your decision. No one else can make it for you. God ordained it so. When you were young, we carried you. We helped you over life's rough places. We thought we led you onward on the path, the narrow path, the path that leads where all of us will want to go. But now the time has come. You have said that you will go away. Tomorrow is the day.

My thoughts go back some twenty years, and sweep and search and grope. If only I could find the seeds [and know] from whence they came, the seeds that separated in your soul and grew and grew and brought such harvest that today we weep.

Your closest friends have tried to tell you not to go. The ministers of your church, ordained of God to answer someday for your soul—they're urging you to stay. Do not go away. We need you, and you need us too.

Perhaps you think when you have left us that we can just tear out your sheet, and all will be as though you never had been here. But you are young, my child. You cannot realize the bonds that bind, and bind, and bind.

Now you say you've found a better way. You want to do great things. You're confident of what you're doing, and you're anxious to go on. Beware lest you become entangled in the snares of this vain world. It promises so much, but in the end it cannot give you what you want.

Now that you are grown up, think of those little feet that follow yours, your little brothers and sisters. See those trusting eyes that look toward you. How can we tell them why you've gone away? How can we explain so they will understand, that you have gone of your own free will? You turned your back on all you once held dear. Your chair is empty at the far end of the table, and no one can take your place.

Sometime there well may come a day when the enthusiasm of your newfound life will wear away. Perhaps the day will come when all this glitter will vanish from your life. Then you may see your highest hopes were nothing, and all the things you sought were vain.

We hope your thoughts will then turn back home, the home where once you, too, were happy doing what you could. Don't be afraid to turn your steps and come on home.

—Anonymous

Lonely and Sad

Response to a mother wanting to know the feelings of others whose children have left home and church:

How do parents feel when children leave home? It is so heartbreaking. At first I cried and cried, and when I got over that, it just made me sick. Still, I had to do my daily work.

Sometimes I feel that I didn't treat them right when they were growing up. I didn't show enough love, didn't talk nice and kind, didn't teach them enough about God and to pray, and so on. Whenever I think about it, such as now when writing about it, it brings tears to my eyes. We can't change what already happened. I will keep praying for them as long as I live.

—*A Lonely Mother*

Sorrowing

We lived on a small farm as renters. Needing more income, it was decided that Dan would work out. When a non-Amish man asked for help, Dad let Dan go. The man he worked for had modern machinery, and Dan soon learned how to run the tractor and then the truck. Soon he was driving a car. By this time, Dan didn't care to stay at home anymore, nor do I believe Dad would have allowed it because of his influence on the other children.

Dad was seriously ill, and his sufferings were severe, but Dan seldom came home to see him. More than once, Dad called from his deathbed, "Dan! Dan!" But Dan did not hear. He was miles away, enjoying the pleasures of this world. Then Dad died.

Dan drifted from one thing to another. He married an "English" girl. Dan never complained, but we think he had many regrets. After some years, we heard that they were going to dances, playing cards, and drinking. I sent them a book telling them how wrong it is to live the life they were living. Later I found out that it only made them angry. Dan loved Mother, although he seldom came to see her. Mother is still watching and waiting, with a prayerful and sad heart. She recalls the sorrow she went through when a little son was laid to rest. Many tears were shed for the innocent little child, but many more tears have been shed for Dan.

I know that today my mother is still sorrowing, not for the one who died, whose body is asleep in the grave, but for the one whose body is still living but whose soul is dead.

—*An Observer*

The following three stories are true, but with names changed:

Andy Zook

Andy was a young, rebellious boy who lived in a community where disobedient children were not allowed to stay at home. After a while away from home, the longing to see the family, especially his young brothers and sisters, grew so intense that he finally mustered enough courage to go home. As he parked the car beside the barn, he heard the door slam. Looking around, he saw his father running with an upraised hammer, straight for the car. He immediately put the car in gear and drove back out the lane. The next we heard of him, he had enlisted in the army, and sad to say, a few of his younger brothers followed him.

—Anonymous

Adam Yoder

Adam was much the same as Andy Zook. One difference was that he could stay at home. One thing led to another, and the time came when he was in trouble with the law. Running through a red light, he struck another car. He was searched, and drugs were found in his possession. When his father found out that his son was in jail, he immediately paid the $500 bail and took him home. What will become of his boy in time, I do not know, but as of yet he has not changed his course.

—Anonymous

Eli Miller

Eli was another boy much the same as the two already mentioned. Although he was not forbidden to stay at home, the sad faces of his father and mother haunted him so much that he didn't spend much time there. After a few years of rebellious living, he ended up in jail for drunken driving. There he had lots of time to think.

His jail sentence expired on a Saturday, and he was free once again. But where would he go? Practically penniless, he knew he would find no friends at the tavern where he had spent so much of his time. There seemed to be only one place to try— home. The sad face of his mother invited him to stay for supper, much like you would invite some special company. After supper, he was admonished that he should go to church the next day, and the relieved feeling at being accepted at home made him think he might go.

However, when he awoke the next morning, that feeling had left him. He got out of bed and looked out the window. To his surprise, his horse, which he had not driven for so long, was patiently standing at the hitching rack, all hitched up. Suddenly the kindness of his parents overwhelmed him. Yes, he would go to church, even if he had to face the people as a jailbird. This was the beginning of a new life for Eli.

Today Eli is a married man with a family. He has often mentioned the sorrow he feels for his wasted years.

—Daniel L. Hershberger

Mother's Musings

Cleaning and scrubbing can wait till tomorrow,
For babies grow up, we've learned to our sorrow;
So quiet down, cobwebs; dust, go to sleep;
I'm rocking my baby, and babies don't keep!

—Anonymous

SIX

Work

FOR READERS WHO HAVE never lived on a farm, the following selections will give you a feel for the Amish love of the land. The Amish are concerned about a future in which fewer and fewer young men become farmers. As land became scarce and expensive, many of the Amish had to turn to other occupations to earn a living. Attempts to go elsewhere to buy farmland and start new settlements were often unsuccessful. In the Lancaster settlement, for example, fewer than half the men earn a living as farmers.

The Amish manage to keep much of the modern world at a distance. But when it comes to work and the technology used to earn a living, run a business, or operate a farm, the Amish have had to adapt, change, and compromise. The use of solar electricity, bottled gas, hydraulics, pneumatics, compressed air, diesel and gasoline engines, and car batteries is now common in many Amish communities. These forms of power may be used in occupations as diverse as dairy farming and furniture making. They have also made their way into the home.

The Amish are asking the logical questions that arise from this work revolution in their communities. As fewer Amish become farmers, will they lose that connection to the land that is so much a part of their culture? Will the rise of Amish businesses, some grossing in the millions of dollars, threaten their very ability to be Amish? While most Americans seek prosperity, many Amish see it as the single biggest threat to their way of life.

Why Do We Farm?

Take paper, pencil, and calculator in hand,
And first punch in the high cost of land.
Add painting, repair bills, and taxes, too,
And sky-high interest that always seems due.
Figure in the long hours that we have to work,
At wages that would make a city guy smirk.
But, oh no! Farming is much more than that!
With our patched-up shoes and our battered-up hat,
And the smell of the stable clinging to our clothes,
To make the nonfarmer wrinkle up his nose.
Farming is the smell of the soil being plowed in the spring,
While the north-flying geese let their music ring.
It's the wobbly legged calf on a dewy summer morn;
It's a good stand of alfalfa, a nice field of corn.
It's the super sweet smell of freshly stacked hay
That fills the entire barn for many a day.
It's a nest of new kittens with fur smooth as silk;
It's a sputnick[1] filled to the brim with warm milk.
It's being your own boss from day to day,
Making your mistakes in your own special way.
It's a soft, gentle rain when you really need one;

---

1 A container for carrying milk to the cooling tank.

It's being up in time to see the rising sun.
It's resting after lunch with the hat pulled low,
Beneath the shade trees where the soft breezes blow.
It's seeing the first corn sprouts pushing through,
Realizing God's promise is still holding true.
As long as the earth remains, it never shall cease,
Sowing and harvest, frost and heat,
Summer and winter, day and night . . .
The march of the seasons so perfectly right.

—David Z. Esh Jr.

Problem Farmers and the Community

A family started farming on one of the poorer farms. After about ten years, they were in such financial difficulties that it seemed they would have to give up. This would have meant selling the farm and seeking employment in town.

At this point, happily, a brother in the church offered assistance. He practically took over management of the farm, dictating to the farmer what to do and what not to do. It must be said to this farmer's credit that he was willing to listen and obey. Otherwise, the plan would never have worked.

In a few years' time, the farmer was once more farming on his own. His family was saved from destruction through the foresight and charity of a fellow church member. Because the farmer was humble enough to accept help, he profited greatly by it.

There is a definite relationship between the farm-oriented family and their support of the Old Order church. No other atmosphere seems quite equal to the farm. Where it is necessary to take off-the-farm employment, the closer the work is associated with farm life, the better.

—Anonymous

Choring Together

I just finished reading about women helping their husbands do the chores in the barn, and how some wives feel a bit like servants. Although it has been quite a struggle, I try hard to be thankful that I am able to help with the work. I am also thankful we Plain people still have the privilege of having our own farms. Just the same, too many times I feel like this poem I wrote:

The Milking Time Blues

The alarm is set every morning at four,
And then it's out to the barn to chore.
The milking's got to be done,
On time—the cows, every one.

Before we're done, the baby's awake,
To cry as though her heart would break.
(When the children wake, how I'd like to be
In the kitchen warm to greet all three!)

Again at four at night, to the barn we go
For another hour and a half or so;
The dishes get left sometimes till late,
And the fussy baby, too, must wait.

I love to sew, to cook, to clean,
To bake, to mend, to fix, to glean;
What fun it is to trim the yard,
And plant the flowers, working hard.

But more important than all the rest,
Are the precious children, all in the nest;

To leave them alone makes my heart ache so,
Especially in winter when cold winds blow.

I shouldn't complain, but my heart's not in it;
I can't force myself to enjoy every minute.
I know we need cows to pay our dues,
But *how* can I shake the milking time blues?

—*A Mother*

Finding a Farm

Probably most of us, if we really consider the matter, would agree that working in factories is not good for building up the church. The following points, as a general rule, do not work for the good:

1. Working with worldly people who practice smoking, swearing, telling dirty stories, and so on.

2. Men and women working together, especially under such conditions.

3. Fathers away from home, many times leaving too early to have devotions with the family.

4. Too much money available. Many people would say they want to work away so they can get started farming, but it seems the number of farmers is getting fewer and fewer.

The list of disadvantages in factory work would be long if everything were included. The good points (for lasting good) are hard to find. There is no easy solution to the problem [of finding a farm], but we would like to make a few suggestions:

1. Spread out. In most of our settlements, farms are available on the edge of the communities at a much cheaper price.

But still the miniature farms are popping up in the center of the settlements.

2. If you want to buy a farm someday, then begin now to live simple and save money. Don't try to keep up with the Joneses (or the Beilers, the Burkholders, or the Millers).

3. In many communities, there is a good market for truck farmers or specialty crops. This could provide profitable employment for the children and can be done on a small acreage.

4. There are always older people who are well established financially. Why not help the young people get started instead of putting money in the bank? Who is it helping if you put it in the bank?

The high cost of living, or perhaps it would be more correct to say the cost of living high, makes it difficult to start farming today and to keep on farming. As far back as we can go in the history of our people, we find they were an agricultural people. In Old Testament days, the Israelites, too, were an agricultural people, as seen by the many laws and commandments given them, nearly all based on a rural people. To change this now would be taking a serious step.

If we consider what effects [leaving the farm would] have on the home and church, the question is before us: Do we really want to change it?

—Sam

Amish Shops

We remember how a few years ago, predictions were being made in some circles that we Amish people wouldn't be able to hold out much longer in our stand against modern farm machinery. The argument was that soon all the horse-drawn equipment would be junked or worn out, and then, "What will you do?"

The last while, one rarely hears those kinds of gloomy forecasts. One reason: we are demonstrating that if something isn't available commercially, there are Amish shops that can make it. If the tool that is needed never did exist, someone will invent and design a tool to do the job. There seems to be a small industrial revolution occurring among the Plain people. We are building everything from buggies to kitchen ranges.

Our foundries melt down chunks of cast iron and transform them into large kettles or tiny harness rings. Leather shops produce harnesses and even manufacture collars. Blacksmith shops turn out plows, manure spreaders, and buggy fifth wheels [metal undercarriage part that allows the front axle to pivot for turning].

A second reason some old-fashioned items are again becoming available has nothing to do with what we manufacture ourselves. It is due instead to the swinging pendulum trends in the world. A lot of people are turning away from the latest technology and are going "back to the land" in an effort to become more self-sufficient.

Perhaps one reason more Amish shops today are manufacturing the items we need has nothing to do with the difficulty of buying the items elsewhere. That reason may be the high price of farmland. Traditionally, the Plain people have encouraged farming, since that was the most logical and suitable place to bring up a family. On a farm, there is always work to be done. Children aren't in the way; instead, they are wanted and needed. Also, children growing up on a mixed farm learn to do many things well, which helps them grow into capable adults possessing varied skills. They learn to do what needs to be done, whether it is delivering an oversized calf or repairing the barn door.

However, with the frightening and almost numbing leap in land prices during the last ten years, a certain number of people have turned to shops and home businesses simply because the cost of farming is too high. They may agree that farming is still the best place for a family if possible, but if not, a business at home is certainly better than a factory job.

—Staff

The Doom and Gloom of Future Farming

The old saying that all a farmer needs is a strong back and a weak mind is no longer true. It is more accurate to say that the farmer needs a broad back and a keen mind—a broad back to carry all the debts, and a keen mind to manage and make wise decisions.

The old people had a saying, "Don't put all your eggs in one basket." This meant that a farmer should have a few chickens, a few pigs, and a few cows. If the price of one goes flat, then hopefully the others make up for it. This is another saying that no longer holds true. It might be better to say, "If you have your eggs all in one basket, you'd better take good care of that basket." It is useless to jump from one thing to another and try to hit the market at the right time. By staying in one thing through thick and thin, a farmer usually has a fairly good average.

There are few young people and even fewer older ones who do not see a danger of working in town for a lifetime. That is why we see more and more home shops and businesses. As the businesses grow, they also provide work for others in the community, giving them a chance to make a living without being in a poor environment.

Then there are the many new settlements starting in areas where the land is cheaper. The young people must realize that if changes have taken place in the life of their parents, they will continue to take place in their own lifetime. The day may easily come when they too will be baffled and troubled because of the future outlook. One old farmer once said, "If a person can't cope with one dry year, he had better not be a farmer, because there will surely be some more."

The important thing for all farmers is to not set their sights on the wrong goals. The words of a song express it well:

> This world is not my home;
> I'm just a-passing through.
> My treasures are laid up
> Somewhere beyond the blue.

> —Anonymous

Rules for Farming

For twenty years, we have tried to emphasize the dangers of modernism, and the spiritual blessings of leading a simpler and plainer lifestyle. At the same time, we have tried to promote consistency, honesty, and openness, basing our life and practices on the principles of the Scriptures.

We say we encourage farming, yet often the church rules are more restrictive for farmwork than for shopwork. That has the effect of encouraging people into shopwork instead of farming. It also has a secondary effect of making many farmers feel dissatisfied with the restrictions that apply to them.

> —Staff

Agreeing on Standards as the Needs Arise

There is no ruling against some things we use today that are just as worldly as other things the *Ordnung* (church rules) has us do without. Certainly a diesel engine powering a sawmill is not less worldly than one that is pulling a plow.

However, as the Industrial Revolution brought changes to all phases of American life, the church responded according to the things that affected the church the most. Since most Plain people are primarily farm people, church rulings had the hardest effect on changes toward progressiveness in the farm community.

In our church standards, there is nothing mentioned about owning railroad locomotives. Of course, Plain people have used railroads a long time for transportation, but no Amishman has ever tried to buy or own one that I know of. Therefore, the question has never been raised. To an outside observer, as well as to some inside, our set standards are obviously impractical. Yet as we know, the *Ordnung* wasn't made in a day, but as the need arose.

As for machinery in shops and small businesses, I believe things like sawmills have always been an important part of a Plain community. On the other hand, tractors and barn cleaners were new inventions in their time. The modern sawmill we see today has been improved through the years. It was not brought into question at any point in its development.

In our church, tractors have been in common use since their introduction. Then when we decided against automobiles, we also decided against the rubber tire. Back in those days, it was not hard to understand, because most tractors came on steel wheels from the factory. Now, however, our young people find it hard to understand that a tractor on steel wheels is tolerable, but that it is "worldly" with tires. I conclude that it is not our *Ordnung* or our adherence to it that is our faith. Instead, *our Ordnung is an agreement* among the church members and not just imposed on us by the ministry, an agreement that certain things may be a detriment to our faith. When we joined the church, we were well aware of this agreement and endorsed it. For our salvation and the redemption of our sins, we depend not on our own works, like keeping a law or rules, but on the shed blood of Christ.

—I. Shirk

The Lunch Pail Problem

We asked our readers to join us in a discussion of the lunch pail problem—fathers working away from their families. As we expected, there are no simple answers.

—Staff

I have just sent my husband out the door with his lunch pail. That is the way it has been for the last four years. It is not the way we would both like it best. We have three boys, the oldest is ten, and they should have their father at home. But we have five acres here, not enough to think of farming. The idea of buying a farm with no savings is not practical. So I guess we will go on as we are for now and hope interest rates and farm prices will come down someday.

—Anonymous

I think the man's personal attitude toward his work and his family makes a big difference and determines whether there is a lunch pail problem. Those who work away from home need to gear their life so they will have several special hours a day together with the family. It can be done. I feel I have seen cases where the busy young farmer did not succeed as well as the happy factory worker or carpenter.

—Anonymous

Here in our new community, most of the families are farming or have shops. There are many blessings to living on a farm. But some of our farms are too big. So Mother is out helping to milk and chore for several hours. In cold weather, the children are alone in the house, with the oldest coping with demands and frustrations. In those families where the father carries the lunch pail, at least the children have one parent who stays in the house with them.

—Anonymous

Solving the Lunch Pail Problem

Here are some ways I have seen families successfully solve the lunch pail problem. Their work is at home. These home businesses are exactly like farming; they must be conformed to church standards. They should not become too large. The livelihood should serve our needs; we should not serve the livelihood. We can become a slave to our farm; the same can happen to a home business. We must not replace the lunch pail problem with a no-time-for-family problem.

Many of the businesses have to hire help, a plus for the young folks who can then work with church members instead of away among outside influences.

A widow and her nearly grown family operate a flourishing poultry-slaughtering service. A husband-and-wife team operate a successful sewing machine sales and service. Another, a bicycle sales and service shop. A young family of eight operate a busy little shop making horse and pony bridle blinds for harness makers. Quality and good workmanship are important if we are to be successful in a home business. We must be competitive.

Other examples are tailoring (making plain suits, etc.), fix-it shops, small-engine services, accounting and preparing tax returns, estate planners, dry-goods stores, homemade bakeries, salvage grocery stores, butchers, sawmill operators, woolen mills, appliance sales and service, alternator and generator repairing, upholstery repairs, manufacturing baskets and bushels, blacksmithing, boat building, bookbinding and printing, selling homemade cheeses and other home foods. People sell and service heavy canvas and timepieces, offer health food services [with bulk foods and home remedies], greenhouses, small nurseries, small foundries (for making buckles, bits, snaps, farm machinery parts, etc.), gunsmithing, binding buggy wheels, manufacturing stovepipes, gutters, and downspouts, and selling air-operated items (such as deep well pumps) and floor covering.

They are also making cabinets, farm equipment (such as flat wagons, harnesses, gates, horse-drawn manure spreaders), mobile homes, sheds, woodstoves and kitchen ranges, pallets and skids (plus repairs), ceramics and glassware, rubber stamps and signs, toy novelties. They run small-animal shops, restaurants, construction projects (trusses, sawhorses, and other wooden specialties); and so on.

—Anonymous

A Priceless Heritage of Faithfulness

Our mission in life is not to go to some far-off foreign land, but to work at home and in our churches and home communities. Our goal should not be to leave behind riches and possessions, farms and homes for our children, but a priceless heritage they will cherish enough to work fervently to pass along to their children. It has been done for generations, and with God's help it can still be done.

—*A Minister*

SEVEN

Church

FOR THE AMISH, WHOSE ANCESTORS in Europe worshiped while hiding in homes or caves to escape persecution, the church is still a community of believers, not a building. Where they gather to worship, there is their church.

Few outsiders ever get to experience an Amish district church service as held in the home of a member. Some non-Amish friends and neighbors have been to weddings and funerals. Yet much of what takes place at church, baptism, and communion services is something an outsider will never see. Writers have described these services in books, often in clinical detail, but they often miss the emotion and feeling of what it is like to be there.

In this chapter we can truly "get inside the heads" of the Amish, share their thoughts, their human reactions, and thus gain a measure of the strength of their faith and community. For those who say the Amish are more worried about religious form and rules than spirituality, these writings offer another view.

Of all the stories I have read in the thousands of pages of *Family Life*, perhaps my favorite is the one titled "Only God Knows." It captures the personalities, feelings, fears, suspense, and emotional release experienced when a new minister is chosen by lot. Here we see the Amish not only as part of a group, but as distinct and very human individuals with hopes, strengths, fears, and sometimes doubts. In other words, they are not unlike you and me.

Children and Church

Church ought to be one place where children are *welcome*. When your little three-month-old baby cries and the one-year-old at the same time, you hear talk after church, "What a racket!" Please, older mothers, why not *help* a young mother with her hands full? She can't nurse the baby and at the same time give the one-year-old his need. Make the mother with a lot of children welcome, even if her babies get fussy.

I've happened to see a young married man chewing gum, not singing, and looking over the church. That bothers me a lot—more than one of the small angels playing—but no fuss is made of that. Every story has two sides to it.

—*Just Another Sister*

Little dolly in a basket, plastic bolt-and-nut set, large and small plastic animals in a pocketbook, plastic folding comb, horse-and-chariot set, tractor, pull-apart beads, book and pencil, small picture books, diaper boxes, plastic case full of midget toys, plastic clothespins, rain bonnet case with candy, steel truck, play money.

You may ask, "Is this a public sale bill?"

No, it is not. It is a mother's supply of toys to keep one little girl's time occupied while church is in session.

Oh! Oh! Here comes Mrs. Dan Erb, and she has that paper bag with toys again. I'll watch so I won't sit near her, or I can't hear Preacher John Lehman.

There comes five-year-old Danny to sit with his sister, and the bench is already overcrowded. I know it doesn't matter too much, because he doesn't sit long anywhere. I see he is already going over to his father.

Opening the door and coming in quietly and in a meek and humble manner is Mrs. Abe Troyer with her little girl. She usually has one string of beads and buttons on a string for her daughter, and the little girl is still satisfied.

What was it the minister once said? "I can see that mothers who take many things to church to satisfy their children seem to have the most unruly ones."

—M.

Hymns and Hymn Singing
The Ausbund

It is a bright, warm Sunday morning. The living room and kitchen of the Yoders' farmhouse are filled with people sitting quietly and expectantly on the wooden benches. The first hymn has just ended, and there is a pause, a moment of rest before the next hymn begins. Then a deep-throated voice from the men's benches calls out, "Seite Siwwahundert und Siwwazig" (Page seven hundred and seventy). There is a wave of motion among the people as they open their songbooks. But there is little rustling of pages. The well-creased books seem to open automatically to the announced hymn.

"O Gott Vater, wir loben dich" (O God the Father, we praise you). The words rise and lower as the leader intones the song. Such a beautiful song, a perfect song to be sung while the ministers are in an upstairs bedroom preparing for the morning service. First God is praised and thanked. Then the singers pray for the ministers, that they may speak God's teachings. Next they pray for the congregation, that their hearts and minds may be receptive to the service. Finally, they ask God to be present during the service. Yes, it is a meaningful song, this second hymn sung at Amish church services.

After a quarter hour, the second hymn ends and the ministers are heard descending the staircase. The members close their songbooks and tuck them away. A little boy, Bennie, is sitting on his father's lap. He reaches down and touches the black book that was just placed beside his father. Bennie tries to lift the book, but its two-inch thickness is too wide for him to grasp. The young man sitting beside Bennie's father sees the little boy's interest in the book. He picks it up and taps Bennie's hand gently and playfully with it. The cover drops open, exposing the title page. The young man gazes at it: *Ausbund das ist Etliche schöne Christliche Lieder (An Excellent Selection of Some Beautiful Christian Songs)*. His attention leaves the open book, for the minister has begun to speak.

The young man did not look at the title page of the songbook for more than a few seconds, but it was long enough for a few questions to enter his mind. He could remember that this songbook had been used ever since he was little Bennie's age. But had it been used when his father was a boy, or when his grandfather was young? Had it, perhaps, always been used in the Amish church? Who wrote the songs, and how long ago?

—D. Luthy

Michael Schneider's Songs in the *Ausbund*

The *Ausbund* is often called in German *das dicke Liederbuch*: "the thick songbook." But that would not have accurately described the first edition printed over four hundred years ago in 1564. It was not thick, nor was it even entitled *Ausbund*.

The first edition of 1564 contained only fifty-three hymns written by a group of Anabaptists known as the Philippites.

They were similar to the Hutterites, living in colonies and sharing all things in common. In 1535 their bishop, Michael Schneider, and some sixty followers left their colony in Moravia because of persecution. They entered Germany, hoping to reach the place where they had lived before moving to Moravia. But the entire group was captured by the Catholic authorities and imprisoned in the castle dungeons at Passau, on the Danube River in Bavaria. During their imprisonment, the Philippites wrote hymns. Michael Schneider himself composed twelve.

After their release from the Passau prison, where all had been tortured but none put to death, the Philippites disbanded. Nothing is known of what became of their leader, Michael Schneider, but some of his followers united with the Swiss Brethren and abandoned communal living. Naturally, they brought with them the songs they had written while in prison. The Swiss Brethren then published the fifty-three Passau hymns in 1564. By 1583, quite a few other songs were added to the original set, and also the title *Ausbund*, which apparently means "special" or "select."

Today the Passau songs are found between pages 435 and 770 of the *Ausbund*, making that section of the hymnal the oldest. While the 1564 songbook contained fifty-three Passau hymns, the present-day *Ausbund* contains fifty.

The Old Order Amish are the only group that still uses the *Ausbund* for church services. Even so, not all the lengthy songs are familiar to the Amish, nor are all the verses of the familiar songs sung. Several of Schneider's songs are favorites of the Amish and are sung at important times. His song "Wohlauf, Wohlauf, du Gottes G'mein" ("Rejoice, Rejoice, You Church of God," no. 97) is sung at weddings. When an excommunicated member reunites with the church, number 99 beginning with verse 20 or 21 is used the first time the person comes to church. Then, when one is received back into full membership, verse 30 is sung: "Es ist auch Freud im Himmel" (There is also joy in heaven).

A few Amish settlements do not use the *Ausbund*. For example, the large settlement in Kalona, Iowa, uses the *Unpart(h) eiische Liedersammlung* (Impartial Collection of Songs), first published in 1860 by Johan Baer of Lancaster, Pennsylvania.

Most people have likely failed to even notice the initials "M. S." at the beginning of Schneider's songs in the *Ausbund*, and some may have mistakenly thought them to stand for Menno Simons. Yet the time Michael Schneider spent composing the songs in Passau prison was not in vain. While his personal fate is unknown, the songs he wrote are still alive today and appreciated by the Old Order Amish.

—Anonymous

In Praise of Singing

Historically, it has been said that the slow singing originated with the Anabaptist Christians. They would sing to their death while being martyred for their faith. In mockery, the people would dance to their singing. Because of this, the Anabaptists started singing slow tunes.

Singing that worships and praises God and spiritually edifies people doesn't have to be sung in four parts, harmonized, or have a musical background. When these things are added to our singing, there is a danger of putting emphasis on the voices and music rather than feeling the message and inspiration the words contain.

Romans 12:2 tells us we are not to be conformed to this world, but to be transformed by the renewing of our minds. This should be applied to our whole life, which would certainly include our mode of singing.

—Orva Hochstetler

Some Thoughts on Singing

What is the reason singing in parts is being accepted in some areas among our Plain people? If we are singing just to see how nice we can sing, we aren't singing to God's honor and glory. When we have our minds on the tune to make sure every phrase works out just right, our mind can't very well concentrate on the words we are singing. Another thing about singing like this is that someone with a better voice can be heard above the rest. Soon that person will be getting praise for the fine voice, forgetting Who gave the voice. When voices blend in the same notes, it will not be so much this way.

—A Young Girl

Singing the Old Songs

Singing the slow tunes as they are sung in Amish churches today is indeed a special assignment. The Amish have kept up and handed down these tunes from generation to generation, for hundreds of years. Singing these old hymns can be likened to the final harrowing before planting the crop. It should help in getting our minds into a prayerful, receptive mood.

Indications are that this type of music grew out of the early Anabaptist church music. Without beat or measure, time or rhythm, it depends upon depth and devotion, appealing to the nobler sentiments of the heart. The song leader sings the syllable of each line alone. Since there are normally two to five notes to each syllable, this can be a major undertaking, especially if he is not well acquainted with the song. The secret of singing any slow tune is to be able to tie the last syllable of each line to the first syllable of the next one.

In most Amish church districts throughout the Midwest, someone is appointed to announce the songs and ask someone to sing them. The Swartzentruber churches go a step further and have a *Vorsinger Tisch*, a table at which the song leaders sit. The *Vorsinger* is usually one of the older brethren who is fairly well acquainted with the church tunes. There may be problems in getting it started. If so, he must be prepared to either start it or ask someone else to start the first line. Then the one who was originally asked to lead will take over. It is the *Vorsinger's* responsibility to decide how many verses of a song should be sung.

Practice singings are held in many communities, where young and old get together to practice these old songs. Most tunes are sung for various hymns and at different times during the year. Most of the counsel meeting and communion tunes are not sung at other times.

Each community has its own variations of many of these tunes. At a wedding, the marrying couple and their families usually decide who is to lead the hymns.

All four verses of "Das Loblied" are sung [the hymn traditionally sung second at most services]. I am always interested to note how long it takes to sing it. Twenty minutes is about the normal time for most Amish communities. For some of the plainer churches, it takes twenty-four minutes, and the Swartzentruber groups may take up to twenty-eight minutes. Many years ago when I was in a Swartzentruber service and was asked to lead "Das Loblied," I soon detected that their tune was slightly different. But what really threw me was when the first and third lines ended up on a different note than I had ever heard before. I thought I had done pretty well in not getting stuck until my host told me on the way home, "Two weeks ago there was a man from Pennsylvania, and he did even worse than you did!"

Since memory cannot be depended upon [to guide rotation], many of the *Vorsingers* keep a card file with the name of each [song leader] on a card. When he leads a song, the date is recorded on his card, and it is put in the back of the pile.

The singing may even have an influence on the sermons that follow. If the ministers appreciate the singing, how much more do we hope that it will ascend and be heard and accepted by the One in whose name we have gathered to worship.

—D. Wagler

Musical Instruments

Musical instruments have been used by popular churches for a great number of years. Those who do so claim they have been of value in promoting spiritual experiences. We should take notice that we have no mention in the New Testament of Christians using instrumental music. On the contrary, we do have Scripture on the evil of music, its natural rather than spiritual effect, prophecy of its condemnation, and use as a shadow rather than the real. "Woe to them that . . . invent to themselves instruments of music, like David" (Amos 6:1, 5). Those who defend musical instruments because they were used in Old Testament worship would have as much Scripture to justify war. The apostle Paul compares spiritual deadness to the sounds of musical instruments (1 Corinthians 13:1; 14:7).

Instrumental music tends to draw attention to itself through its natural beauty, distracts our thoughts from the meaning of the words we sing, and entertains us rather than glorifying God. Also, instruments of music are an expensive luxury. Much money is wasted that could be put to better use.

—Anonymous

Baptism

The Amish practice what is called "believers baptism": that is, baptism occurs for those who are old enough to understand, believe for themselves, make lifelong vows, and be accountable. According to custom, applicants for baptism among the Amish are at least sixteen years old.

Is It Merely Joining the Church?

Why would anyone want to join church without being born again? [I hear various comments.]

"My friends are joining church, so I want to also."

"I'm grown up, and my parents and relatives keep bothering me until I do. Then when I have joined the church, the pressure will be off, and I can do more as I please."

"My parents want me to be baptized so that if anything happens to me, I can go to heaven. I don't want to go to hell, so I better join church, and then everybody will feel better."

When I was taking instructions for baptism, there were several in my group who were not permitted to date until they were baptized. On the evening of the day of their baptism, all of them dated. How sad that they should cast a dark shadow of suspicion upon their motives for being baptized.

Applicants for baptism have been seen coming for instruction dressed in immodest clothes and wearing unbecoming hairdos. Yet they claimed they were saying no to the world.

When such things are seen, is it not a sign that the Christian faith has degraded into a Christian culture? Anyone who is born again will live for Christ, but those who are merely living a Christian culture are living for themselves.

When we are born again, we have the desire to be in fellowship with others of God's children. The ceremony of baptism has been given us so that we can testify to the church as well as to the world that we are now God's children. We are members of Christ's body, the church. Joining church is a consequence, not a cause. It should be the result of a change of heart, instead of being considered the change itself.

—David E. Miller

Proper Preparations for Baptism

Can water make a Christian? Can church membership make a Christian? If it were possible to make Christians by simply baptizing them, then we should do as they did in the 1400s— use the sword and force people to be baptized, or run mobs through a river like a German king did. We realize that this would be ridiculous and not scriptural. Exactly what did our ancestors believe in the line of baptism and church membership? Menno Simons writes, "We are not born again because we are baptized, but we are baptized because we have received the new birth. He who seeks remission of his sins through baptism rejects the blood of Christ and makes water his idol."

If we wash the bowl only on the outside, but not on the inside, we will never be anything but worldly, sinful, wretched, miserable, poor, blind, and naked (Revelation 3:17).

—Anonymous

Faith, Works, and the Anabaptists

The Anabaptists were strict on the conduct question. Unless applicants showed evidence in daily life of being born again, they simply were not baptized or accepted as members. A tree is known by its fruits. Christianity is a practical thing.

Because the Anabaptists were practical, they soon had a reputation as "good" people. Even their enemies, who persecuted them, admitted that their conduct of life was more holy than for any other group. The Anabaptists became so well known for their good works that anyone who rebuked sin or left off sinning was at once suspected of being one. In the same way, people were sometimes cleared of Anabaptist charges by their bad behavior.

—J. Stoll

The Holy Kiss, Sacred Symbol of Love

What exactly is the purpose for the holy kiss, and what does the Bible teach about it?

In 1 Thessalonians 5:26, Paul says, "Greet all the brethren with an holy kiss."

The kiss was a common secular greeting of that day, but the Christians practiced a special version of it, the holy kiss. What made it holy? It was sanctified, first of all, by the devout lives of those who practiced it. Second, it was imparted with a prayerful blessing: "Peace be with you" or "God be with your spirit."

The holy kiss is rooted in history. The Anabaptists practiced it. Menno Simons mentioned it in his writings. Today almost all Amish churches retain traces of it, proving that it was once universally practiced by the Plain people. Those traces vary from community to community. In most places, ministers still greet each other. Other communities have retained a bit more, and the ministers greet each other plus the older members. Other communities go still farther, with the ministers greeting each other and all other members.

In some churches, it is practiced as Paul commanded it: all members greet each other, regardless of age or calling, the sisters greeting the sisters, and the brothers greeting the brothers. We believe in practicing the holy kiss because it is a Bible-commanded symbol of our spiritual bond of love.

The holy kiss is a sacred command, one of the most meaningful symbols of love and goodwill that exist in the world today.

God forbid that we should either continue to neglect it, or permit it to become an issue of contention and disunity among the very people it was meant to unite, the children of God.

—E. Stoll

Footwashing: Our Dusty Feet

The practice of footwashing, as Jesus commanded in John 13, is one of the Bible's most neglected and forgotten doctrines. If so many churches don't practice it, why do we? This is much more than just an outdated practice carried over from Bible times. The doctrine carries a deep and important spiritual meaning for the Christian church throughout all the ages and in every culture. Its spiritual meaning is twofold:

1. The practice of [paired and reciprocal] footwashing among the entire brotherhood dramatically underlies Jesus' revolutionary concept of humility. He chose the most extreme example of servitude. He, their Lord and Master, stooped to wash the dusty, sweaty, smelly feet of common fishermen and tax collectors! No king before ever had such an idea of how a great ruler should reign over his subjects, by serving them! Our world today, as greedy, haughty, and self-serving as ever, still needs that truth demonstrated.

2. The second spiritual lesson taught by footwashing is that we still *do* get dusty feet. We may not always get them physically dusty, but it was the spiritual dust Jesus was most concerned about anyhow. Jesus spoke of two washings, that of the feet being one, and of the hands and head and the rest of the body being the other. There is the washing that occurs when we are first converted [a full cleansing]. The second washing, that of the feet, signifies removal of the dust we pick up from our daily walk of life. Our weak flesh, our dusty feet, need daily washings. We cannot expect to walk through this world and not get some of it on our feet.

To stoop at communion service and wash the physical feet of my brother [or sister with sister] is not nearly as hard as the spiritual washing it symbolizes. When I see my brother [or sister] in an error, it is my duty to go to him and with love and goodwill and above all humility, tell him about it, and admonish him. Ah, that is the true footwashing.

Our attitude toward our brother [or sister] must be that of a servant, feeling ourselves of less importance than the one whose feet we wash, the one whose error we help to overcome.

There is no room for the holier-than-thou feeling here. Washing is gentle, washing is cleansing. Some of us, when we see a brother in error, forget to wash, but go for the cleanup job with a wire brush. There are certainly plenty of dusty feet, but the servants willing to stoop and wash them are hard to find.

—E. Stoll

Leaders in the Church

Being a minister in an Amish church is a heavy responsibility, as ministers receive no salary or compensation. They must simply add their ministerial obligations on top of their regular occupation, family responsibilities, and daily life. These selections offer a window into the weight of ministerial responsibilities.

A Survey of Amish Ordination Customs

Several years ago an Amishman who had just been ordained bishop was congratulated by his non-Amish neighbor. The Amishman was dumbfounded, not knowing what to answer when congratulated. No one else had ever congratulated him, but many brethren had wept with him. The Amishman, like any newly ordained Amish bishop, wept. The burden of his office felt too heavy.

Amish ordinations, whether for deacon, minister, or bishop, are solemn and serious affairs. Amishmen do not attend a seminary seeking ordination. They do not seek it in a political way. They never ask to be ordained. It is thrust upon them by lot. This practice of ordaining by lot is based on Acts 1:23-26, where lots were cast to see who would replace Judas as the twelfth apostle.

When he joins the church, every Amish boy knows there is a possibility that he may someday be ordained. In fact, in most Amish settlements, the bishop asks the boys who are joining church whether they are willing to accept the ministry if the congregation should someday ordain them. Their answer must be yes, or they cannot be baptized.

The full count ["full bench"] of ordained men in each Amish congregation is considered to be one bishop, two ministers, and one deacon. When the bishop feels the congregation is in a position to hold an ordination, he announces so two weeks before the *Ordnungs Gma* [church counsel meeting, a semiannual service in preparation for communion]. This two-week period is called *Besinn-Zeit* (time to think it over and pray about it). Most congregations require that the members be 100 percent agreed to hold the ordination. The ordination usually takes place two weeks later, on communion Sunday. [Each district holds services on alternate Sundays, as listed in Ben J. Raber's *Almanac*.]

[After the communion service, usually,] the bishop in charge stands and says a few words about the seriousness of the occasion. He then reads 1 Timothy 3. (In some areas, Titus 1 is also read.) The bishop does not specifically mention that the person must be a married man, but such is taken for granted.

When the qualifications have been mentioned, the bishops and other ordained men leave the congregation and go into an adjoining room of the house. One ordained man (often the deacon) remains with the congregation to see that all the members come forward one by one to say who they feel should be in the lot. Another ordained man stands just inside the ministers' room, with the door slightly open so as to hear the name whispered to him by each member.

Each [baptized] member of the congregation goes to the door, men and boys first, then women and girls. Each time the minister at the door receives a name, he closes the door and repeats it to the bishop in charge, who then writes it down. Each time the same man's name is mentioned again, he places a mark beside it.

Each Amish congregation has its own rule on how many *Stimmen* (voices, votes) are needed to place a man in the lot. Some congregations require two, while others require three. This is based on Matthew 18:16, where Jesus said, "In the mouth of two or three witnesses, every word may be established." No members, even husbands and wives, are supposed to discuss for whom they are going to vote.

The average number in the lot in a large congregation is around eight; four is an average number in smaller congregations. The presiding bishop determines which men are in the lot, takes an equal number of songbooks, and places them before him. Inside one of the books, he places the lot, a slip of paper with German writing on it. (In Lancaster County it reads, "The lot is cast into the lap; but the whole disposing thereof is of the Lord" Proverbs 16:33.)

In Lancaster County, a large table is used, and the men sit around it with the songbooks in the center. When all are seated, they reach for the songbooks, one by one. In some areas, they take the books beginning with the oldest man first. In other places, it is done in the order their names were announced, in the order in which they received the required *Stimmen*. [Next, the bishop examines each book.] Once the bishop comes to the book containing the slip, he reads the words on the slip and says the man's name so all the congregation can hear.

Only ministers may advance to [be ordained as] bishops. Generally [if there is no bishop in a district,] there are three ministers, and usually all three are included in the lot [for bishop]. But in Lancaster County, there is a major difference from anywhere else except the daughter settlements [of people from Lancaster]. Verses 4 and 5 of 1 Timothy 3 are more strictly applied. To qualify for the lot [for bishop], each minister must have children who are church members, or at least one child, and all their children must be in good standing. Deacons are ordained by lot in the same manner as ministers.

Their duties, however, differ. A deacon is in charge of the *Armengeld* (money for the poor), enforces the *Ordnung* (rules) by talking with disobedient members, counsels couples wishing to marry, reads Scriptures at the church service, and gives *Zeugnis* (a testimony) to the sermons. In most Amish congregations, he does not preach. In some areas (such as Lancaster, Lawrence, and Mifflin Counties in Pennsylvania, among others), the deacon's office is looked upon as so strictly separate that he may never leave it for [other leadership] ministry.

If the lot is cast, it is up to God to see where it falls.

—D. Luthy

Only God Knows

Who, oh who would it be? The ministers had just come in, and now the old, white-haired bishop had arisen. He stood before the congregation. "Those chosen in the lot are . . ." His voice faltered and he paused. He needed a moment to steady his voice. His heart went out in sympathy to the brethren whose names were written on the paper in his hand. How solemn this ceremony was, this choosing of God for a man to preach the Word!

Most of the men sat with lowered heads. William Yoder shifted his feet. Before he was married, he had been reckless and defiant. He had done some deeds that he now longed to erase from his mind forever. It was true, he had settled down later and gotten married. He was a concerned husband and father. But it was not easy to live with a burdened conscience. After services, he would watch [for] his chance and talk with one of the ministers or a bishop. It no longer mattered that he might have to make a public confession. He was more than willing. He sighed. Life sure looked different at twenty-eight than it did at eighteen!

The bishop cleared his throat. His voice was steady once more. Slowly, clearly, he read the names. "Mark Miller, Joseph Mullet, Amos Mast, William Yoder, Henry Graber, Dan Yoder." After a long pause, Bishop Ray said, "You may come up here on the front bench." Six black books, each bound with a rubber band, were lying on the table in the front of the room. In one book was a slip of paper containing an appropriate Bible verse. The man who drew that book would be the one chosen by God.

Through a blur of tears, Sylvia Mullet saw the men take their places. Surely it would not be Joseph! How well she remembered her father's life. He had been a minister and had had such a burden to bear. How often he had been blamed for things he had left undone or had done wrong. More than one night, she had awakened and knew by the light of the lamp in the kitchen that he was sitting at the kitchen table, with his Bible before him.

The knowledge that she was a preacher's daughter was always with her. There were many things she could not do that other girls did. Dear, dear Joseph. Must it be him? And what about herself? How unworthy and unfit she felt to be a preacher's wife. She twisted and untwisted the handkerchief in her hands.

Henry Graber sat with his head bowed. For months he had had this feeling. Perhaps God was sending him a warning that he would die soon. At night he would wake up, and the feeling was there. He reviewed his life. Was there something in his life that God was not pleased with?

Then the bishop had announced that a minister would be ordained, providing the congregation felt agreed and prepared. Was this what God was calling him to do? Henry tried to shrug the feeling off, but the thought persisted. "Prepare yourself. Prepare yourself." Over and over these words rang in his mind. At night he had wrestled with this feeling. Human eyes did not see the battles, the silent but real conflicts that raged within his breast.

The bishop was talking. He had laid the little black hymn books on the table. Only God knew which book had the slip of paper. God would lead and guide. He made no mistakes. The Lord would give grace and courage to the man he chose. "Let us kneel and pray," the bishop said.

There was a shuffling of feet, and then all was quiet as the people knelt. The bishop's voice had been steady and quiet, but now as he prayed it trembled.

Sylvia Mullet felt numb. She heard the bishop's voice, but to her shame she realized later that she had not heard a word of the prayer itself. Then the bishop was standing. "You may come and draw your books," he instructed.

Stand up, go over to the table, and pick up one little book. It seemed like such an easy thing in itself, but Dan Yoder had never realized how hard it could be to do such a small thing. He was a fearless man, unafraid to stand up for his beliefs. But now in this solemn moment, his courage and strength seemed to have left him.

William Yoder's blue eyes were dark and troubled. "Unworthy, unfit, unprepared," he thought. He lowered his head, and tears dropped on the small black book in his hands.

Henry Graber's face was very pale. "He is working too hard," the people said. And yet there was no one more willing to help others when the need arose. He often left his own work to help his neighbors.

Joseph Mullet looked very young as he drew his book. His brown eyes were clear and trusting. Joseph's mother tried to swallow the lump in her throat. Joseph had always been an obedient son. Tenderhearted, quiet-spoken Joseph.

More than one person had the feeling that the chosen one would be the bishop's son, Amos. Now his usual friendly look was replaced by a burdened look. How well he knew the load his father had to carry!

Mark Miller, his curly, bushy hair looking disorderly, picked up the last book. Only God knew the thoughts that went through the minds of the six men on the front bench. Only God knew which man held the book with the slip.

Now the time had come. How can a person describe the tension, the strain, and the silence that was felt at this time? For weeks this moment had been looming before them. It had been wondered about, prayed about, struggled with. Within a few short minutes, all wondering, all doubts, all questions would disappear. God's choice was about to be revealed. Yes, there was a strain that could be felt. But there was also a feeling that God was with them.

The bishop walked over to Mark Miller. Carefully the rubber band was taken off his book. Quietly, carefully, the bishop paged through the book. The rustling of the pages could be heard in the back of the room. The book was returned to Mark. He was not the one.

Next was Joseph Mullet, the youngest in the lot. He felt weak. His hand trembled so that he felt unable to give his book to the bishop. Sylvia sat with her head bowed. When she forced herself to glance toward Joseph, the book had been returned to him. He had not been chosen.

Next was Amos Mast, the bishop's son. Bishop Ray's hands trembled as he opened the book and paged through it. The slip was not there, so the book was returned.

Only three remained. The bishop's face was pale. He suffered with the men before him. How he could feel for them!

Would it be William Yoder? He was next. The slip was not found in William's book.

Now there were only two men, Henry Graber and Dan Yoder. Which one would it be? The bishop reached for Henry's book. How quiet the room was! The pages of the book rustled. The bishop cleared his throat, followed by another silence. "The Lord has chosen Henry Graber."

The congregation saw only the man with the bowed head. They did not see the turmoil of feelings inside. They did not know how relentlessly the good and evil had striven within his breast. They did not know how hard it had been for Henry to give up his own will and accept whatever it was that God had called him to do.

To preach the gospel, to help keep the church pure and unspotted, to visit the fatherless and widows, to help the sick and needy, to rebuke and admonish the sinners, to live a life that would be a shining example of the gospel. Yes, it might mean to be blamed and misunderstood, to be accused of showing partiality and picking on certain members. It would undoubtedly mean spending sleepless nights and leaving his dear wife and children with lonely evenings, when his duty called him away from home.

One of the ministers was speaking. How well he knew the truth of the words uttered to the solemn, listening congregation. "You can help to make this a tiresome, heavy burden that God had placed upon our brother today, or you can help make it a great joy in his life."

A burden or a joy? Which would it be?

God had done the choosing, but now the answer to this question did not lie in God's hands alone, but in the hearts and lives of his people. A burden or a joy. Which would it be?

—Anonymous

Letter to a New Minister

I would like to write this letter to you while the scene from yesterday is still fresh in my mind. I am sure all of us will cherish for many days that experience when you were ordained as a fellow minister in our church district.

How short the day seemed. I know that many people in the world pity us when they hear that our services last for three hours. I wonder what they would say if they knew a service such as yesterday lasts up to eight or nine hours. While the outside world continued on its way, we met to worship, to partake of communion, and to ordain a minister.

Today is another day. Today we go about our work. We milk the cows. We harness the horses. We fill the silo, haul the manure, or plow the soil. For most of us, life slips back into a familiar routine and goes on much the same as it did before.

For you it is different. You awoke this morning to a new world. The sun arose for the first time upon you as a minister of the gospel. Your life will never again be the same.

Many thoughts have gone through our minds since yesterday. Yesterday we spoke a few words to you, and wept a few tears with you. But our tongues were too tied, our vocabulary too incomplete to be able to express the yearning in our hearts. How inadequate words seem at such a time. Mostly we could just sit and share the time with you in silence.

Yet words have their place. In the days to come, those words will return to you. You will recall comfort and support whispered to you that the rest of us didn't hear. You will remember that God has a purpose in each move he makes, a master plan he is seeking to fulfill. We often can't understand. Sometimes it doesn't even make sense to us. But God doesn't ask us to understand. He only asks us to believe, to trust, to accept, and to submit. "God is his own interpreter" [from the song "God Moves in a Mysterious Way," by William Cowper]. In his own time, he will explain when he is ready and, perhaps more importantly, when we are ready. You did not seek that calling. But I trust you will not shrink from it either.

In our humanness, we would have liked to come to you and comfort you by telling you that the task was not as great as it looks to you. But to do so would have been wrong. God does not want us to make the task smaller in order to make it bearable. But the Lord does want us to let his grace become greater in order to make the task possible.

Overnight, in fact in one hour, your responsibility has been greatly increased. You have been taken from the sheep and placed among the shepherds. You have been lifted from the residents of the city and set up as a watchman upon the walls. You must move fast enough, but not too fast. You must be firm enough, but not too stern. You must be patient, but not too patient with the wrong things. You must decide when to act and when to wait, when to speak and when to be silent.

Do not forget that your wife shares your calling with you. She cannot escape a share of the responsibility. At this time, she too needs to be comforted, needs someone to speak words of courage and strength to her. At a time when you need her to help you, you find she needs your help instead. It is often those in life who need the most help themselves who can be the greatest help to others. God's "strength is made perfect in weakness" [2 Corinthians 12:9].

Satan will tell you it is not fair that you should be the one. He will try to make you rebel when you need to take a Saturday afternoon off to study or instruct applicants for baptism while your neighbor gets his oats cut. It will not seem fair that your neighbor can go ahead and get his chores done while you stand and explain some church decision to a member who questions the decision. The same is true when your neighbor eats a good warm bowl of soup after a hard day of work while you skip supper because the deacon came to take you with him on the thankless task of visiting an erring member.

To make matters worse, your neighbor will get up the next morning, rested and refreshed. It will not make it any easier to realize that some of the problems that kept you awake are the result of mistakes you yourself made along the way. These may be things you said but shouldn't have said, and things you didn't say but should have said. Despite such things, God is not a hard master. Not only is God fair, but you will find that members in the church will do their part too. It is true that some may sleep while you preach, but others stay awake and listen. Some may cause you extra cares, but others will do their utmost to lighten the burden, showing their appreciation. I will never forget the neighbor who came over one afternoon to help me with my work, for no other reason than the simple explanation, "You often have to work when we don't."

Yesterday one of the ministers said to you, "Welcome." I can think of no word more fitting with which to finish this letter. Welcome into a new family. The ties in a family are formed by the trials the family faces together, by work they share, by joys experienced and difficulties surmounted. The ministry is such a family.

We know that you will not always agree with us. You will even discover that we do not always agree with each other. We try to live above our personalities, our petty grievances, our human weaknesses, and to work united by a common goal greater than ourselves—the welfare of the church. Often we fall short, but always we go back and try harder.

No one knows the weaknesses of other members of the family better than do the members themselves. But if the family is as it should be, each member still loves the other. We challenge you to lose yourself in a labor of love. Only then can you be truly worthy of the calling through which you were called.

There is work to do, challenges to be faced, mountains to be scaled, enemies to be conquered. God has been good to us all. *Welcome.*

—Anonymous

EIGHT

Discipline

FEW AREAS OF THE AMISH FAITH are more misunderstood than those of discipline in the church, excommunication, and shunning. Newspaper stories focus on the tragic tales of those under "the ban" from the point of view of those being shunned. Hollywood movies find shunning great dramatic material, exaggerating it to incorrectly show the Amish refusing to talk to or even look at shunned persons.

Shunning does indeed result in sad separations of family members, and it's a painful process for all involved. Yet there is a reason behind it. The Amish themselves admit it is not always "properly applied." From the beginnings of the Amish faith in 1693 and right up to the present, shunning has played an integral part in preserving the Amish way of life.

Here then is a look at shunning, how it is carried out, and why, from the Amish point of view and in their own words.

Church Discipline
Discipline in the Church

The teaching of excommunication (*Bann*) and shunning (*Meidung*) was an important point to our Anabaptist forebears. They saw that the state churches of their time, whether Catholic or Protestant, did not have a scriptural concept of a disciplined brotherhood. The Anabaptists believed that the true church of God must be a disciplined church, kept pure from sin and worldliness. The church should be made up only of sincere believers who live holy lives.

The Anabaptists felt that the state churches failed at both ends—in how they received new members (by infant baptism) and in not expelling those who failed to live holy lives. I believe most of the disunity today that is said to be about *Bann* and *Meidung* is about something else.

The present-day Old Order Amish churches can be divided into roughly two camps on the *Meidung* question: those with a policy of "*streng* (strict) *Meidung*," and those without it. By *streng Meidung*, we mean a policy of excommunicating and shunning a member who has joined a more liberal group. (The exact line may vary as to how much more liberal [the joined group may be], but is usually drawn at the ownership of automobiles.) The rationale for this is usually that the member is breaking the baptismal vow, loves the things of the world, and shows a spirit of discontentment.

The Amish-Mennonite division of 1693 comes to mind. When Jacob Ammann and Hans Reist parted company, one of the points of contention concerned how *Meidung* should be observed. The Amish faction felt that expelled members should be shunned to the extent of not even eating an everyday meal together. The Mennonite factions felt that Paul's words— "With such an one, no not to eat" (1 Corinthians 5:11)—meant not to partake of communion with such a person. This difference can still be found between the main groups of Old Order Mennonites and the Old Order Amish of today. Interestingly enough, the gap has narrowed over the years.

If a member has moved from a church without a *streng* policy, he would also usually find himself excommunicated and shunned [by his church of origin], and basically for the same reasons. The difference comes when the member has proved himself [as being built up in the faith] at his new church and is living in peace there. Then, providing that the new church is basically the same in important points of doctrine, and also with regards to the working of the Old Order church to the extent of formally "lifting" the *Bann*, the erring member then ceases to be shunned by the Old Orders.

It should be pointed out that in each camp described above [strict shunning contrasted with milder discipline], there exists considerable variation.

This brings us to the crux of the matter: Is there one true church, or are there many? That was the real issue in Jacob Ammann's time. Could the "true-hearted" find salvation in the state churches? Time has a way of bringing changes. It is now three hundred years since Reist and Ammann had their differences about the "true-hearted." Among the Amish, there are few groups today, if any, who believe in only one true church in the way Jacob Ammann did.

The issue between the *streng Meidung* camp and the others is not a question of *Meidung* as much as it is of whether we recognize those other churches as true or not. Of course, God is the final judge. But it is my understanding of the Scriptures that a church should excommunicate only those they feel will miss salvation unless they repent. Too many churches are playing with the *Bann*, treating it as though it were a light and trivial matter.

It is surely high time that we stop comparing ourselves with those in the opposite camp, which Paul says is not wise (2 Corinthians 10:12). Instead, we should compare ourselves with the Word of God, and the standard set therein for the church. The place to begin is to make sure that we ourselves are what we should be so that the churches may be purged and renewed.

—E. Stoll

Three Great Walls

Many worldly people, and perhaps some church members too, have mistaken the purpose of the *Bann* and avoidance (1 Corinthians 5). The church is not to use the *Bann* as a wall to keep members from escaping. As in any discipline, some members, when they see what happens to those who err, may well fear to follow the same path. However, the primary function of the *Bann* is to keep the church pure.

The *Bann* punishes the evildoer not in the spirit of revenge, but to bring him to repentance. Used in this way, the *Bann* expresses in the strongest means possible the church's love and concern for the erring member's soul.

—J. Stoll

Church Divisions

Nine Principles for Mending Broken Relationships

Two basic things can happen that cause broken relationships in a Christian community: someone sins against you, or you sin against someone else. Any sin, however small, that causes disharmony must be dealt with. Here are nine principles based on Scripture that will help us mend broken relationships:

1. Confess to the Lord.

2. Make the first move.

3. Do it quickly.

4. Meet the person face-to-face.

5. Go in genuine love.

6. Go in the spirit of peace and reconciliation.

7. Confess, apologize, and ask for forgiveness.

8. Let this end the matter.

9. Forgive your brother again and again.

—Anonymous

Submitting to Each Other

Many splits in the past have been the result of people putting a lot of emphasis on certain points or doctrines. Many of these doctrines have been good and necessary in themselves. The danger resulted from promoting them so aggressively that a church split resulted.

We tend to forget that the Bible also teaches that we are to submit to each other, to esteem others more highly than ourselves, to walk in love and consideration for our brothers and sisters, and to be meek, patient, humble, and teachable.

—D. Luthy

Shunning: A Discussion

The following discussion of shunning is arranged in question-and-answer form. For many of the answers, we have quoted from the writings of our ancestors on this subject, especially from Menno Simons.[1] Menno was the most outstanding leader among the persecuted Anabaptists in the Netherlands during the sixteenth century. He wrote much and traveled extensively, teaching and preaching.

---

1 Quotations from *Dietrich Philip's Handbook* (Pathway Publishers, 1966) and *The Complete Writings of Menno Simons* (Herald Press, 1956).

What is meant by shunning? The German term for shunning is *Meidung*. It refers to the practice of refusing to have social or business dealings with a person who has been expelled from one's church. It is applied to the extent of not eating with the person under the *Bann*. Another term for shunning is *avoidance*.

Upon what Scriptures is the practice of shunning or avoidance based? There are a number of Scriptures which support shunning, but it should suffice to list here the five major ones:

1. Matthew 18:15-18. In these verses, Jesus explains the pattern to be followed in disciplining an erring brother. If the brother remains unrepentant, the matter must be made known to the church. "But if he neglect to hear the church, let him be unto you as an heathen man and a publican." Now the Jews to whom Jesus was speaking were totally separated from the "heathen and publicans." They had absolutely no dealings with them, did not eat with them, and in fact were reluctant to step inside their houses.

2. The second passage is the entire fifth chapter of 1 Corinthians. The report had reached Paul that the Corinthians left undisciplined a man who "had his father's wife." In this chapter, the apostle Paul earnestly commands them to "put away from among yourselves that wicked person." Once the church has "purged out" such a person, Paul explains further what their relationship should be toward him. "But now I have written unto you not to keep company, if any man that is called a brother be a fornicator, or covetous, or an idolater, or a railer, or a drunkard, or an extortioner; with such an one, do not eat."

3. Second Thessalonians 3:6. "Withdraw yourselves from every brother who walks disorderly, and not after the tradition which he received of us."

4. Titus 3:10. "A man that is an heretic, after the first and second admonition, reject."

5. Romans 16:17. "Now I beseech you, brethren, mark them which cause divisions and offenses contrary to the doctrine which you have learned, and avoid them."

Did our forebears believe in shunning? This question can best be answered by quoting from the Dordrecht Confession of Faith. This confession was drawn up in Dordrecht, Holland, in 1632, and was signed by fifty-one Mennonite ministers. It was adopted by [Swiss Anabaptist ministers in the Alsace in 1660 and kept by] the Amish [from their division of 1693]. Article 17 says:

> As regards the withdrawing from, or the shunning of, those who are expelled, we believe and confess that if any one, whether it be through a wicked life or perverse doctrine, is so far fallen as to be separated from God, and consequently rebuked by and expelled from the church, he must also, according to the doctrine of Christ and his apostles, be shunned and avoided by all the members of the church (particularly by those to whom his misdeeds are known), whether it be in eating or drinking or other such like social matters. In short, that we are to have nothing to do with him, so that we may not become defiled by conversation with him and partakers of his sins, but that he may be made ashamed, be affected in his mind, convinced in his conscience, and thereby induced to mend his ways.

What is the purpose of shunning? Dirk Philips, a bishop and coworker with Menno Simons, taught that the purpose of shunning is threefold:

> First, that the church may not become a partaker of the strange sins, and that the little leaven, leaven not the whole

lump (2 John 1:11; Gal. 5:9; 1 Cor. 5:6). Second, that the person who has sinned may be ashamed and his flesh be mortified thereby, but his spirit saved in the day of the Lord Jesus (1 Cor. 5:5; 2 Thess. 3:14-15). Third, that the church of God be not evil spoken of on account of wicked members in it, and be not censurable on their account before the Lord (Ezek. 36:17-24; Josh. 7:20).

Concerning the first of these three reasons, Menno Simons writes in greater detail: "The lepers were not allowed among the healthy in Israel. They had to stay in segregated places until cured. O brethren in the Lord, the leprosy of the soul is a leprosy above all leprosy, whether it be in doctrine or in life. It eats like a canker."

Has not the question of shunning caused a lot of trouble in the churches? Shunning is a practice commanded and sanctioned by God for the protection of the church. The obeying of God's commandments brings a blessing to all involved, not trouble. But what has caused trouble in the church has been people who were no longer satisfied to accept what God has ordained.

The question of shunning has caused trouble in the church in the same way as have other Bible doctrines the worldly mind finds hard to accept: nonresistance, nonconformity, modesty in dress, prayer veiling, subjection of women, and footwashing. All of these and many others have been haggled over during splits and divisions because some members wanted a closer walk with the world. Shall we put the blame on the doctrine or on the worldly thinking that can no longer submit to it?

Is it not true that shunning is done at times in a spirit of revenge and out of spite toward the person shunned? This is all too true in some cases and is to be deeply regretted. When the need arises to discipline an erring member in the church, the ministers and the members should pray earnestly that they might act out of love and concern, and never out of ill will or spite.

Are not wayward members driven farther away from the church by shunning? If they remain unrepentant, it is well that they are driven far enough away so that their influence does not harm other members.

Would many not repent sooner if they were not shunned? Evidently not, or God made a mistake when he commanded shunning as a means of bringing about repentance (2 Thessalonians 3:14). Sadly, today the reason shunning in certain cases is not more effective is the hypocritical way it is carried out. When the entire congregation stands united and consistently admonishes and rebukes the erring member with deep sorrow and love for his soul, it becomes a powerful force in moving him to repentance.

However, much of this power for good is lost when some of the members, although not actually eating with the banned member, seek every opportunity to be in his company and laugh and visit together as though nothing were wrong. It is a reproach to the church and a mockery before God when members obey only the letter of a commandment, but disregard the spirit.

Should shunning also be practiced between husbands and wives, and between parents and their children? Menno Simons answers:

> First, the rule of the ban is a general rule and excepts none, neither husband nor wife, neither parent nor child. Second, we say that separation must be made by the church, and therefore the husband must consent with the church in the separation of his wife, and the wife to the separation of the husband. Third, we say that the ban was instituted to make ashamed unto betterment of life. . . . Spiritual love must be preferred to anything else. Fourth, we said the ban was given that we should

not be leavened by the leaven of false doctrine or of impure life by the apostate. It is plain that none can corrupt and leaven us more than our own spouses, parents, etc.

Although Menno here advocates shunning between husband and wife, he also recognized that this matter was laden with great danger and needed to be handled with consideration.

Are we allowed to show the banned persons needful services, love, and mercy? We are not only allowed but commanded so to do. It is our duty to help anyone destitute and in need, even if they are our bitterest enemy. Menno Simons says, "The Scriptures do not forbid these, but they forbid common daily intimacy, conversation, society, and business. The ban is a work of divine love and not of . . . cruelty."

When the Bible says, "Have no company with them," does that forbid a friendly greeting when we meet? Once again, we cannot improve upon the answer that Menno Simons penned over four hundred years ago. "Good manners, politeness, respectfulness, and friendliness to all people becomes all Christians. . . . How can such a one be convicted, led to repentance, and be moved to do better by such austerity? The ban is not given to destroy, but to build up."

Should members ever be shunned before they are expelled from the church? Menno's answer is no. "It is not the custom or usage in Scripture to shun anyone as long as he is carried and tolerated in the church. Therefore, we should not shun anyone before excommunication, for if we do, we practice a ban neither known nor mentioned in the Scriptures."

How serious should the ban be considered? Very serious indeed. Menno Simons said the ban is a death certificate of our souls. He wrote the following words only three years before his death: "I would rather allow myself to be cut into pieces until the day of judgment, if that were possible, than to allow myself to be excommunicated according to the Scriptures, by the servants of the Lord, from his church. O brethren, take this seriously."

We have already quoted so much from Menno Simons that we may as well let him add the summary to the article. After reviewing at length all the Scripture passages that teach shunning, Menno says, "I verily do not see how a God-fearing heart can oppose in regard to this matter. There are such good fruits and benefits contained in this shunning. But it seems that this vine must always have its harmful worm."

—E. Stoll

The Story of Demas

Written to a person excommunicated and under the ban:

You have been admonished time and time again. But you have still chosen to forsake us and leave us for a closer walk with the world. The only course left for us was to excommunicate you from the church and now practice what scripturally follows that excommunication: the ban and avoidance, which goes with it.

The human nature in us does not want us to do so, but we have so much Scripture to support that doctrine that we cannot do anything else. Your way of life and your beliefs are no longer a help to us, but could even be deceiving to us and to others. We will therefore have to limit our dealings with you.

We know that some of you who have left us are saying that avoidance and separation are surely not the way of love. Our answer is that if we have a neighbor who is not even a church-goer and who we know lives in gross sin, we will not hold the ban against him. We act this way because we are not to judge those who are without, but we are to judge those who are within (1 Corinthians 5:12).

God knows that nobody can be more of a deceiver than someone "called a brother" who has fallen away and starts to live a life of sin (1 Corinthians 5:11). That is why such a one is to be separated from the church, so that he does not have as much influence to mislead others. If you are one who has caused "divisions and offenses contrary to the doctrine which ye have learned," we must mark and avoid you (Romans 16:17).

We did not first reject you. You have rejected us and the way of living that we value and hold dear. There is not to be a trace of hate in the practice of the ban.

—Anonymous

Our Life Is Different

Comments by a woman whose husband left the Amish faith:

We never discussed his leaving the church; he just went. What a shock it was! I am so ashamed to say that I did as Satan wanted me to do: I quit praying. There were no arguments between my husband and myself, but I was drifting right along with him, although I still went to our church. Then God held me back from taking that step [of leaving the Amish].

Our children have never known what a true Amish home life is like. They've never had their daddy in church. How much easier those first years could have been had he only had more love for us than for his worldly things. I have many faults and could so use the help of a Christian husband, but it's not to be. Some things are easier to live with as time goes on, but this isn't one of them. It seems so hopeless. Yet where there is life, there is hope. My husband says he wishes he could come back, as I wish he would, but adds, "I can't."

Living like this often makes me feel unwanted, and I feel I'm not really a part of the church. We have never been able to hold church, though the children have often asked when we, too, can have church in our home.

If it would accomplish anything, I could sit and cry about it all, but life must go on. Crying helps, but brooding doesn't. Depression is something I have to work very hard against.

It also makes our children feel different. They often get pushed back. Not all people make us feel this way. We have many friends, probably more than we realize. But often on the holidays during the week, others will be invited somewhere for dinner and our children ask, "Why aren't we?"

In closing this article, my wish is that even though you don't know us, please pray for us. Without the prayers of others, we couldn't go on.

—Anonymous

We Set the Example

We had scraped together enough to buy a farm of our very own. It was a large farm, and we were very busy. One day I came to the realization that things were not progressing as they should to make a go of it. What was to be done? I spent many sleepless hours pondering the problem. We simply had too much to do. If only we could have some of the labor-saving devices and equipment, we could get back on our feet. The farm was too large to be run the way the regulations of the church required.

A plan formed in my mind. I talked it over with my wife. At first she was aghast that I would consider joining a more liberal church, but gradually I got her to see things my way. While I was trying to convince her, I was trying to justify myself.

The people dressed plainly in that church. They seemed very concerned to live a Christian life, and very sincere. They welcomed us warmly to their church services. The day came that we changed over.

Everything went as planned until our children joined church and wanted to be like the other young people. We found that the young people didn't dress as plainly as we'd thought, or else they'd changed. If our children wanted to have friends and mingle with the young folks, they had to dress like them. So we compromised a little.

Time went on. One by one the children married and left home. Sometimes when I saw how different their life was from what my youth had been, my conscience pricked me and I spent a restless night. But I pushed these thoughts aside.

Then one day the announcement came that made me see everything in its true light. It was a complete shock to me. Our second eldest son and his wife were leaving "our church" to join a still more liberal church, a church that allowed short skirts, television, small head coverings, and lately even divorces. My wife and I tried to talk them out of it. We pled as earnestly as we could, but they had made up their minds.

"Can't you see the pitfalls in such a liberal church?" my wife asked with tears in her eyes.

"Oh, we're not going to allow a TV set in our home," our son replied. "We and the children are going to dress the same as we always did. It's just that your church won't allow the long-distance trucking that is becoming a necessary part of my job. We feel we'll be able to serve the Lord more fully this way."

With that, they left.

—Anonymous

NINE

Clothing

WHEN YOU'RE AMISH, the whole world knows it. That is
because of the unique plain dress. In some ways, this effort to show
separation from the modern world and a lack of interest in worldly
fashions has put the Amish into a fishbowl. Their nonconformity
in dress attracts the interest and curiosity of those around them,
especially in areas frequented by the touring public. Stories abound
as to why the Amish dress as they do, and many of these are pure
conjecture.

Ironically, the world sometimes finds the simplicity of Amish
dress to be fashionable. In the early 1990s, *Vogue* magazine fea-
tured "Amish fashions" with slender, blond models photographed
in Lancaster County. Several Amish saw the photo spread and were
either shocked or amused by what they saw, not to mention the
price tags!

Most Amish do not know much of the history behind why they
wear what they wear. For them, their plain clothing is simply their
way of doing things. Here are excerpts that provide some background and insight into the origins and importance of Amish

clothing. They also relate fascinating experiences its wearers have had with their dress in the "outside world." These, then, are the words of the people who wear the clothes.

The Bible Talks about Dress

The Bible talks about dress from the fall of [humanity] to the end of time [Genesis 3; Revelation 19:8]. Sinful man continually designs fashions that are not pleasing to God. God designs clothes to cover the body, not display it. Men and women are to have different types of clothing. God's people in Old Testament times were to wear a peculiar and distinctive and uniform garb.

Nothing is to be worn for show or pride or vain display. The Christian woman is not to have her hair cut, or put up in worldly hairdos. The Christian man's hair is not to be long like a woman's. Combing the hair according to worldly styles comes under condemnation. Harlots' clothes are red and purple. Jewelry is forbidden.

The effectiveness of Christians' testimony depends upon their appearance. People with renewed minds do not walk as they formerly did.

—Anonymous

The Accepted Pattern

I hope I wear my broad-brimmed hat as a protection against the weather and also because it has been the accepted pattern down through the ages among our people. But if I do these things, or drive my horse and buggy to show off, then there is pride in my heart, and I cannot expect a blessing from it. However, if I do it because I feel it is right and fitting for a nonconformed people, then I believe it can be a part of living my faith and living *by* faith.

—D. Wagler

Reasons for Wearing Plain Clothing

There are several reasons for wearing the kind of clothes we do. The first reason, of course, is for modesty's sake, because we want to wear the kind of clothes the Bible says we should wear rather than what the styles and fashions of the world tell us.

Another reason is that we would rather be identified with the children of God than the children of this world. It seems right and proper to us that soldiers wear a uniform to show that they are a part of the army. Bus drivers wear a certain uniform, as well as many others, such as nurses, and so on. Why then should it be unusual for religious purposes?

Outward adornment is forbidden. Since jewelry serves no useful purpose, we believe it is forbidden. But the wearing of clothes does serve a useful and needful purpose; therefore, it is not forbidden. But adorning ourselves by the clothes we wear is what is forbidden.

Since women are not to cut their hair, it becomes necessary to do something with it, such as braiding or using some other method to keep it under control. Therefore, this serves a useful purpose. But we are not to adorn ourselves through plaiting the hair any more than we are to adorn ourselves by the clothes we wear. We believe it is the adornment that is forbidden, not the plaiting of hair. Even gold may be worn if it is for some useful purpose, such as dentistry work.

—Staff

Head Coverings and Bonnets

The Anabaptists wrote little, if anything, about the women's head covering. The eighteen articles of faith [Dordrecht, 1632] do not even mention it. The reason for this is not that they did not believe in it, but because they lived in a day and age when the head covering was not questioned. Until even a hundred years ago, no decent woman, let alone a godly one, would have appeared in public without a head covering.

Our historical library contains a clipping from a 1940 *National Geographic Magazine* showing an old woman in her home in rural France. No doubt she is Catholic, but her head covering looks so similar to an Amish cap that you would think she was Amish.

—Staff

An eighteen-year-old woman whose mother had passed away asked if she should wear a prayer covering at night. Over three pages of replies were printed! Even more were sent in. Here is a typical answer.

Wearing a Prayer Covering at Night

First Corinthians 11:5-6 teaches that a woman while praying or prophesying is to have her head covered, covering her long hair. Worldly women display hair for sex appeal to the eyes of lustful men. With her covering, a woman signifies acceptance of her place in God's order, lest she dishonor her head (man), and in turn dishonor God, who gave this command.

A special promise for obedience to God's command is given to women in verses 10 and 15: power from God and glory in long uncut hair. My answer to the question is that God sees obedience to his commands both day and night.

—L. K.

Wearing a Prayer Covering in the Hospital

I was a patient in a hospital, and every day the nurses came to change the bed clothing. One day when they came into my room, I was still in bed and had my head covering hanging on the bedpost. One of the nurses remarked to the other, "She's got her religion hanging on the bedpost."

This brought shame to my face. I felt guilty for not having it on. From then on, I resolved that they would not see me again with my head covering anywhere but where it belonged.

Since then, I have been at the hospital a few times and have always kept my resolution. I have also been at the hospital to visit others. When I see their coverings lying on the bed stands, it brings back memories of the lesson I learned.

—Anonymous

What Does a Bonnet Look Like?

[A woman wrote of her bus trip. During an overnight wait in Philadelphia, she couldn't sleep because passengers from arriving buses kept asking her to watch their suitcases for them.]

When I had time to think over my trip, I wondered why all the different people had singled me out from the crowd. I believe it was because of my plain clothes and bonnet. They never asked me if I was a Christian. They took that for granted.

Perhaps some girls or women will read this who are reluctant to wear plain clothes and a bonnet. Don't be ashamed of these things. The world trusts you and takes it as a sign of a Christian. Live up to their expectations, and then your bonnet will be beautiful indeed.

—Mrs. Wayne Miller

Dresses

Only Yesterday

In general, a midcalf skirt is considered modest enough in most of our Plain communities. Just take a look through a fashion magazine of fifty or sixty years ago and compare the length of the skirt with what most Plain women are now wearing. There is quite a difference. Just think, if the average Plain woman was transported back in time to 1910, she would be looked upon with great shock and amazement. "Look at how short her dress is," they might say, and she might even be arrested. And these would be "worldly" people who would condemn her.

The point is this: somehow over the years, Plain women have been following after the world with regard to dress. They have lagged behind current styles, it is true, but have nonetheless been following along. Let us restore the modest, concealing attire worn by chaste women of old. Let us get rid of the signs of compromise which have crept into our plain garb almost unawares.

—S. S.

Why Wear a Cape?

In our Old Order Mennonite churches, it is customary [for women] to wear a cape [an extra piece of material over the front of the dress). But the practice is being questioned. I have heard mothers who were unable to explain why it should be worn.

I understand that some think it is an unnecessary article, just a hangover of tradition. But let's not miss the point. In 1 Timothy 2:8-9, Paul says, "I will . . . that women adorn themselves in modest apparel." Now the word *modest* is defined as chaste, decent, unpretentious.

Without a cape, we make an unnecessary show of our figures. Girls may not realize that they are tempting others to impure thoughts. The Bible teaches that the lusts of the people corrupt a nation.

By immodest dress, we are a hindrance to others. But by modest dress, we can be a help to each other to think pure and holy thoughts.

—I.

Beards

The War of Whiskers

Let us take a look at beards in the Bible, in history, and among us today. There can be little doubt that in Bible times, God's people wore beards, not so much from religious convictions, perhaps, as for the same reason they wore eyebrows—simply because it was the natural thing to do. Yet in the Old Testament, we do find instructions forbidding the Israelites to shape and trim their beards according to heathen customs (Leviticus 19:27).

During King David's time, it was considered a terrible shame and embarrassment not to have a beard (2 Samuel 10:4; 1 Chronicles 19:5). Removing the beard in Bible times also carried a symbolic meaning, indicating a state of deep distress and shame, loss, or defeat (Isaiah 7:20; 15:2; Jeremiah 48:37). Of the twenty times the word *beard* appears in the King James Version, in nineteen instances *beard* is translated from the Hebrew word *zaqan*, which included all the facial hair without making the modern-day distinction between the mustache and the rest of the beard.

We feel that Bible principles and common sense support a consistent wearing of the beard. First is the principle of sex distinction, the belief that the confusing and blurring of a clear line between man and woman is wrong. "The woman shall not wear what pertains to a man" (Deuteronomy 22:5). Facial hair is a common mark of masculinity.

The second major biblical principle supporting the wearing of a beard is the teaching that the creature should be in subjection to the Creator. When a woman uses lipstick and eye shadow, we say she is not satisfied with the way God created her. Is not the man who shaves off his beard to make his face soft and womanish guilty of the same thing?

If we study history, we find that the beard was a point of contention in the 1690s between Jacob Ammann and Hans Reist, the leaders in the Amish-Mennonite split of 1693. Actually, not the beard, but merely the trimming of the beard was the point upon which they disagreed. The trimming and stylish shaping that Hans Reist permitted was the beginning of the end. Reist's followers eventually lost the beard entirely.

Today there is much reason to believe that the beard is once more threatened. There are still bishops living in some of our largest and oldest settlements who in their younger years required unmarried boys who were church members to wear beards. Today, no doubt many or perhaps most boys in those same communities think that unmarried Amish boys have always been smooth-shaven.

Not only is the trend to wait until married or longer to let the beard grow, but Amish beards are shrinking in size and in length. The loss of the mustache brought with it Abraham Lincoln beards. Now the Lincoln beards are being replaced with neck beards. The next step will be no beards. What does being married have to do with wearing a beard? Or by the same token, when we give the right to shave off three-quarters of the area of our face where God causes hair to grow, why is it so wrong to take off the other quarter?

—E. Stoll

What Does Our Conduct Show?

Some years ago my wife and I, along with another couple, were traveling and came to a big city where we had to spend the night. As we walked up the sidewalks, we saw a man standing, weeping, with tears running down his cheeks.

He said to us, "When I saw your women, I had to think of my mother. She always wore a shawl and a bonnet, just like your women do."

As he talked, he was weeping. I had to think, "If our women had been dressed in the present-day garb with shorts or miniskirts, where would this man's thoughts have gone?" Never to his old mother. The garb of our women probably talked louder than the modern-day evangelists are talking.

Once when we wanted to get on a train, the conductor said the seats were all filled, except in the club car. He said we would either have to sit in the club car or wait for the next train. We did not know what a club car was, so we got on.

As we entered the car, people were drinking, smoking, playing cards, and whatnot. But the atmosphere soon changed. The seats in this car ran lengthwise along each side of the car. As we seated ourselves, there was a man on the opposite side who had a bottle in one hand and a cigarette in the other. He could not face us. He glanced first one way and then the other, and looked like he was going to faint. Soon he picked up his smoking stand and went to the other end of the car.

Soon a lady came to us and asked us what she must do to be saved. She was told to "believe on the Lord Jesus Christ, and you shall be saved" (Acts 16:31). Why did she come to us, since we were total strangers to her?

When she left, others came and asked questions concerning our faith. This went on from seven in the evening until around midnight. We were busy answering questions out of the Bible. So the club car wasn't so bad after all.

However, we can also be a hindrance to people if our conduct is not according to our garb. A preacher once related that at one time he lived close to town. He learned that the townspeople called the Plain people "the Pharisees." He could not understand this and decided at the first opportunity, he would ask the townspeople why.

As he was thinking this over, he remembered how some of the Plain people were not always living an orderly life and were drinking and smoking. He finally decided, "If they don't say anything to me, I won't say anything to them about being called Pharisees."

May the Lord help us in our everyday conduct that the light of his presence may shine through us so that others can see that we are his followers.

—P. M. Y.

The Blessings of Obedience

We wear plain clothes, but we know plain clothes do not save us. We give alms, but our good works cannot earn the grace of God. We partake in communion, but know that the emblems in themselves are just bread and wine, with no power to sanctify us. We pour water at baptism, and know the water cannot wash off a single sin. We obey because God said so. Is that not, after all, the best reason, the most important reason in all the world?

—E. Stoll

Living Our Faith

We believe our children should not wear fashionable clothes or cut their hair according to style, but do we explain to them why? How many of us realize that the rules and regulations of the Plain churches are designed to protect us from the evils of the world?

To dress in simplicity will not necessarily put humility into the heart. But if our young people dress in plain and simple clothes, will they look right to walk into a theater, bowling alley, or like place? Would a man with a beard and black hat look right sitting in a tavern, taking strong drink?

We may have convictions against certain evils. But are we willing to teach our own children according to these convictions, if that would cause them to stand out from the crowd?

—Henry Hochstedler

TEN

The World

SOME PEOPLE ARE UNDER the misconception that "the Amish live today the same way they did three hundred years ago." While their way of dress and "horse culture" may seem frozen in time to us, it is obvious that the Amish have changed a great deal. Anyone who has recently visited an Amish home in Lancaster County can attest to that.

Nevertheless, the Amish do not change as often or as much as the world around them. They attempt to limit and control change rather than have "progress" run away with them. It is sometimes a rocky road to travel, but in many ways they have been successful.

It has been said that the Amish are often as curious about us as we are about them. Here is a look at how the Amish view the modern world around them, and also how they are viewed by others.

A Baby to Pity

Freda Bender propped herself up on her elbow and surveyed the hospital room where she lay in bed. The only other occupant in the room was Mrs. White. Freda turned her head toward the door as a nurse came in with her baby boy. A second nurse followed the first with Mrs. White's baby.

The poor little boy! What kind of world would he be taken home to? How could a boy grow up surrounded by dancing pictures on the TV screen, a world of smoking and drinking, a world of gadgets and switches and concrete sidewalks? What chance did he have of growing up and really amounting to something?

Suddenly Freda stopped, seized by a new thought. Was it possible that Mrs. White was also pitying Freda's little son? Was she saying to herself, "Poor little baby! He's doomed to grow up in that primitive way of life. All he'll ever have a chance of being is a common farmer, toiling with his hands, sweating all his life, deprived of so many enjoyments—no car, no television, no chance to go to college, no chance that the poor fellow will amount to much."

There was no doubt that the two babies were born into homes that were different from each other. Baby White would grow up in a world that put a premium on good looks, brains, money, recognition, and pleasure. Baby Bender would grow up in a world that put a premium on character, conscience, morals, and serving others in love rather than trying to get on top.

—E. Stoll

The Power of Suggestion

We are asked, "What! You don't have TV? What do you do in the evening?"

The first time I was asked that question, I was stumped. What *did* I do? I had never realized this was a problem. Yet this man made it sound as though there was nothing else to do except watch television.

Once again, it would make more sense for us to reverse the question, and be asking, "What! You mean you have time to just sit and watch television? Don't you have anything more challenging, more worthwhile than *that*? When do you get your work done? When do you visit your friends? When do you read good books? When do you tell the children a story, or help them play a game, or put a puzzle together?"

Instead of stammering around when asked how we can get along without television, we might better be asking them how they can get along *with* television. How do they cope with all that violence their children watch? How do they expect to teach their children good values? How do they hope their children will grow up and not have minds that are warped by all the immoral and trashy programs?

—E. Stoll

Court Ruling Recognizes Amish Way of Life

[A well-written article quoted the 1972 U.S. Supreme Court decision, "The state does not have the authority to force Amish parents to send their children to high school," and commented:]

The court saw the religion of the Amish as a "way of life," and that their everyday living is regulated by what they believe. This is in direct opposition to the popular churches, many of whom believe that their religion is something to be lived on Sunday. Naturally, it presents a challenge to us to live the kind of life as set forth in the opinion of the court. Are we really worthy of such an opinion?

We have no guarantee that, if a similar case were brought before the court within several years' time, the opinion would be favorable. Nor do we need to depend on the opinion of the Supreme Court or any other court. Our Anabaptist forebears suffered persecution and even martyrdom rather than going against their understanding of the Bible. If the Supreme Court would have ruled against the Amish in this case, then it is doubtful whether the decision would have influenced many Amish parents to send their children to high school. True, they may have had to accept the consequences, and be branded as criminals, or had their property confiscated. Or they may have migrated to other states that are more favorable.

In short, we are thankful for a favorable decision, and we should strive to live up to the opinion of the court as far as our educational standards are concerned. Yet we should not allow it to influence us in becoming slack in our standards. What we do, we should do to serve God, not man. We should be diligent in providing a satisfactory education for our children because we believe it is the right thing to do, and to train them and bring them up as the Bible teaches, in the "nurture and admonition of the Lord" [Ephesians 6:4].

—Anonymous

Fighting for Freedom?

Recently, my wife and I were waiting in a depot to board our bus. We noticed a man with a large emblem on his coat: U.S. Marine Corps. He was soon joined in conversation by another man, who asked him how long he'd served in the Marines. For a few minutes the two discussed their involvement in Vietnam. Then the marine said, "I think everyone should be willing to serve their country and fight when necessary."

The other man agreed, but then commented, "Yet war is a bad thing and not right."

"Of course war isn't right," the marine agreed. "But it's our duty to fight to preserve our freedom when an invasion comes. The trouble with our country is that we have too many cowards, too many draft dodgers, even people who want to be religious. They dress differently and look down on those who go to war to fight for our freedom. They think they serve the good

Lord by not fighting." I was now beginning to realize this man was really speaking to me. "By refusing to fight, these people weaken the very structure of our country. If they don't want to fight for our country, they should all be thrown out. Junk is what I call them."

I was somewhat aghast at this man's vehemence as he expressed himself. I was still thinking about him as we boarded our bus. Is it really true that the strength of the nation lies in having the biggest guns and the bravest soldiers? Or does it not lie in the Christian homes and churches? Is the nation free because of huge arms and defenses, or is the nation free because God in his goodness has chosen to bless the nation with freedom? In one day God could take that freedom despite all the arms in America.

America has freedom, yes, and it is something we should daily thank God for. Yet Jesus, when he was here on earth, taught his followers not to fight. He never talked about becoming free from the oppression of cruel or bad governments here on earth. But he did talk about becoming free from a spiritual kingdom—that of Satan.

Is America then free, with a moral disintegration of society, the rise of corruption with divorce and remarriage, fornication, drinking, drug abuse, theft, murders, hate, strife? The list could go on. No, America is not free. Yet Jesus spoke of being free from sin. He has the answer: "If the Son therefore shall make you free, ye shall be free indeed" (John 8:36).

—David Bender

Thoughtless Zeal

I suppose we've all been guilty of being more zealous than thoughtful. There's an old story that I understand is true, illustrating what I'm trying to say. It proves that no matter how right or how righteous we may be, if we use faulty thinking to support our position, we're not going to be very convincing. This is the way I remember hearing it:

An Amish brother was walking along the road toward town. A car came along, slowed down, and stopped. "Want a ride into town?"

"Sure thing."

The car was soon on its way again. The driver was a stranger to the Amish, and he was curious. Between puffs of the cigarette he was smoking, he began asking questions. He found his passenger friendly and talkative. Before long, the driver reached for another cigarette. He held the pack to the man seated beside him. "Here, want a smoke?" he offered.

"Uh, no, I don't smoke. I don't believe in smoking," the brother answered. Then he laughed a little self-consciously and continued. "You see, I figure God didn't intend that man should smoke. If he had, he would have built him a chimney."

The driver didn't say anything for a moment. Then he braked the car and brought it to a stop.

"I'm sorry, sir," he said. "You can get out here. I suppose if God had intended that man should drive, he would have put him on wheels."

This may sound like a joke, but it really is not. There's a deep principle here. We must be careful to base our faith on the Word of God and not on human reasoning.

—J. Stoll

Outsiders, Tourists, and "Seekers"

Seeing beyond Culture

My wife read to me your article on tourism in Lancaster County, Pennsylvania. I listened with interest but also with sadness. The sadness that comes to me is because so many tourists are seeing the Amish [merely] as a culture. I do not believe the Amish could have endured as they have for three hundred years if there were not a deeper reason for not changing with the world.

This is especially true in a place like Lancaster County, where the Amish are encircled by the industrial complex. Their prosperity itself would long ago have exterminated their culture. In other American groups, the German dialect, or any other dialect, failed to survive much shorter periods than this, thanks to the pressure of the society about them.

What then makes the Amish click? It is their faith in God. Of course, we know that the Amish are not perfect in all their practices, and they have room for improvement. But their sustaining power is their belief and understanding of Scriptures concerning nonresistance, nonconformity, divorce and remarriage, worldly education, separation of church and state, nonjoining with worldly churches, and their theology. These are the things that have kept the Amish from drifting and becoming swallowed up by the worldly culture around them.

—Anonymous

Telling about the Faith

A man said that he had always thought the Amish people were not friendly. But now that he had met some, he didn't find it that way at all. It is true that when we are driving down the road and someone tries to take our picture, it is hard to be friendly. So many people are interested more in our customs and culture than in what we believe. Because of our dress, we attract attention. Instead of rushing away, we have a good chance to tell them about the faith that is within us [cf. 1 Peter 3:15].

—Monroe Beachy

How I Tried to Get Rid of the Rude

The most unpleasant experience I ever had with photo hunters was several years ago. I had my horse hitched to the surrey and had four or five of the children with me. We were going to my sister's house. My nerves were tense as I turned north, for I always dreaded this one mile on a U.S. highway.

At first it wasn't too bad. We had gone about half the distance when a car passed me. "Tourists," I said when I saw how they looked back and watched us. Then they turned around and approached us slowly from the rear. I saw they had a camera ready. "Put your heads down," I told the children on the front seat, and I also put mine down. They stopped beside the road in front of us. We passed them, and I urged my horse on. I watched for the car to pass us again, but they stayed behind us until the highway was clear from both directions. Suddenly the horse jumped, and I saw they were passing us on the wrong side. When they were in front of us, they suddenly pulled across the road in front of us. I pulled the lines up tight, hoping none of the children would slide off the seat because of my sudden stop.

Suddenly I realized they had us where they wanted us. I couldn't put my head down because I had to control my horse, and the children were too curious to see what was going on. I felt anger rising up inside me and, before I knew what was happening, I was yelling at them, "The nerve of some people!" I don't know if I shook my fist or not, but at least I almost felt like it.

Of course, just at that moment the camera clicked, and I could see they greatly enjoyed my annoyance. Right away I felt ashamed of myself. I checked both ways for traffic and drove past without looking at them. They soon went around us again, and this time they were laughing and waving their hands mockingly as they sped away. What kind of witness had I been to these people? Would it make them respect the Amish more? And what did God think of me? Just because they were rude didn't make it right for me to be the same.

Maybe God lets things like this happen to try us out. I have also found out that not all tourists are rude and disrespectful.

Several years ago one evening, my husband and I were at the sale of a friend of ours in town. A man and a woman came out, and the woman asked, "Would you mind if we took your pictures standing beside your rig?"

"We'd rather not," answered my husband.

"Thank you," said the lady. "We just didn't know."

We looked the other way and started walking toward the alley. My husband said to me, "They'll probably get us anyway."

I couldn't resist a glance backward and was surprised to see them walking away. They had respected our wishes and didn't take any pictures.

Human nature being what it is, I suppose we will always have the politely interested, the curious, and the rude people. But I hope, with the help of God, I will never again lose my temper when I meet the latter kind.

—Anonymous

Letters from Non-Amish Readers of *Family Life*

I am neither Amish nor Mennonite. But this does not mean that I disagree with what you believe, nor does it mean that I regard your faith as "simple and primitive." It simply means that I was born into a family of another affiliation and have not as yet changed.

I read *Family Life* because I enjoy learning about the people I believe are closer to Jesus than any other people on earth. There are a great number of "outsiders" who admire you for the fortitude and courage displayed in living your lives for Christ.

As a child in Lancaster County, I often saw the "strange people" in the little black buggies. As I grew older, I began to wonder, "What makes these people give up the luxuries of life to pursue a life of humility and hard work?"

Often I asked questions about the Amish, but those I asked knew no more about you than I did. So I began reading books about the Anabaptist movement and about the development of the Anabaptist faith. However, these books were written by scholars whom I felt did not reflect the true nature of the Amish people.

At this point I began to realize that I did not really want to know *about* you; I wanted to *know* you, a people who would voluntarily choose to become members of the Christian community. I wanted to know people who would not give up merely one hour on Sunday to worship God, but would devote their whole lives to being Christians. So I subscribed to *The Budget* to learn what I felt would give me values to base my own life upon. Through *The Budget*, I learned of *Family Life*. Now I feel I understand basically what you believe in, and at least in my mind I am able to share and enjoy a magazine that I feel helps me to be a better Christian.

So you see, sir, there are many of us outside your faith who believe yours is the way of Christ, and we want to know about your faith so that we, too, might become better Christians. We want to learn about you so that our lives might resemble your lives, our families might resemble your families, and our love of Christ might resemble your love of Christ.

—Ronald V.

I am a convert to the Amish, and I would like to write a few lines to those people who "didn't have enough time to stop and answer some unbelievers' questions."

I am glad someone took the time to "talk" with me. At first they did not have to say one word; their lives did the "talking." I feel this is the main way in which God called me out of the world into his kingdom.

—Anonymous

"Outsiders" Joining the Old Orders

One of our local ministers said recently he was having a conversation with an Old Order Mennonite about their experiences with "outsiders" wanting to join the church. Later, when the newness wore off, they tended to leave again. When the Amish minister learned that this Old Order Mennonite group uses English in their church services, he commented how they don't have the language barrier like the Amish do. But the Old Order Mennonite man shook his head and said, "If they're sincere, they'll learn the language."

I think most Amish are willing to speak English any other time a group includes somebody who does not understand the German.

I have a good friend who some years ago was an "outsider" and then made the changeover to the Amish church. It was a struggle for him, but I think he is now fairly well adapted to his present way of life, and he has been an inspiration to me.

Don't ask us to be like the people mentioned in Revelation 2:14-15, conforming to the world in order to win it. I think this is quite popular nowadays, and God hates it. To all outsiders, if you see good works from the Amish and your heart is yearning to know more, go and visit a minister or anybody [Amish] you know. They should be able to help you a lot, even if you can't understand German, if they can talk with you personally.

—Daniel L. Hershberger

What Others Think of the Amish
Hypocrites?

It is a sobering thought to think that the only members of our congregation that many worldly people come into contact with are those who are not living the faith. The logical conclusion is for the world to decide that if these are hypocrites, then we are all hypocrites.

—Staff

Envying the Plain People

Today there are people in the world who are tired of their sinful living. Perhaps they envy the Plain people for their simple living and try to imitate them in many ways. They will plant their own gardens, sew their own clothes, heat their home with a wood-burning stove, and may even go to live in a cabin in the woods.

However, all these things without the true faith in God are but clinking cymbals and empty shells. We all know what happens to the hippie type of commune started by the people of this world, in an attempt to live together in love on their own strength.

When people of this world want to join our groups, we ought to be careful to explain to them that the plain and simple life in itself merits us nothing. We should emphasize that the way of faith is the way of the cross, of self-denial, obedience, and self-discipline.

It is true that we are promised many blessings in this life. We are promised food for our bodies, clean air to breathe, clothing to cover our nakedness.

Yet these are only fringe benefits. The real reason for serving our Master is because he has loved us with an everlasting love and called us to be children of the Most High. The promise he has given us is that through sorrow we can have the peace of God in our hearts, even in this life, and after this life we can be partakers of his glory in eternity.

—Anonymous

Amish in Magazines

Today it is not at all unusual to pick up a magazine and discover an article featuring the Amish. As the gap widens between the simple Amish way of life and the push-button American society, more and more attention is focused on the Amish. Americans likely view the Amish with much the same regard they are showing high-priced antiques, as something that contains part of their own past, a heritage they have left for modern living, yet cannot help admiring.

—Anonymous

Living Up to Our Reputation

Has there ever been a time in the history of the Plain people when we have received so much favorable publicity as today?

We know that many of the things they are saying about us are not really true, at least not for many of us. They say we put God first and do not live for worldly pleasures, yet you and I know we fall short in this. The pursuit for the dollar and things money can buy is much too common. They say how peace-loving we are, how gentle, kind, and forgiving. You and I know there is too much ill will and gossip, too much strife and backbiting and hate, and too many church splits. They say we lead clean lives, yet in some communities the sins that should not once be named among us (Ephesians 5:3) have become much too common.

They say we are farmers and people of the land, and yet we have entire church districts where hardly a farmer can be found. They say we are careful with the soil, conscientious conservationists. Yet when it comes to drenching the earth with poisonous sprays, some of us keep up with our non-Amish neighbors. They say we have no juvenile delinquency. Yet in entire communities, the majority of the young people spend their weekends in drinking and rowdy living, so that at times police have had to be called in to restore order.

Against such a dark picture, lest we despair, we need to remember that there are entire communities where most of these evils are unknown.

A group of Amish men were working together, repairing their schoolhouse, when a newspaper man stopped in. He asked for permission to take some pictures. When the men declined, he insisted a bit.

"But what about all the bad things people are writing about you that aren't true?"

"The bad things people say about us that aren't true won't hurt us," the Amishman replied. "It's not in our place to worry about that. Our task is to just make sure the bad things they say *aren't* true!"

—E. Stoll

ELEVEN

Aging, Illness, and Death

EVERY SOCIETY AND RELIGION must deal with illness, aging, and death. The way each handles these can tell us much about that culture, its beliefs and values. In the Amish faith, the separation of church and state is clear; they traditionally accept no Social Security benefits and take care of the older folks themselves. Sometimes the grandparents live in a separate section of a house, added onto the home. Living with in-laws and grandchildren has its joys and challenges.

Sometimes brothers and sisters take turns caring for an ill parent. Communities often rally to help pay a friend's costly medical bills. Times of trial can make people stronger or destroy them.

Death is the ultimate test of faith. It may be awaited with fear or a calm acceptance. The Amish deal with all of this within the framework of their family, the community, and their belief in a life yet to come.

When the Young Grow Old

When late autumn strips the leaves from the trees around us, we can see the distant regions that were hidden from us all summer. In the same way, old age may rob men and women of earlier enjoyments, but it is only to enlarge the prospect of eternity. Old age is a threshold.

Listing some of the problems and discussing them may help our older brethren and sisters to be better understood and appreciated:

- We are still tempted.
- We don't have anything to do.
- We don't feel needed.
- No one takes our advice anymore.
- We get blamed for spoiling the grandchildren.
- With only ourselves to care for, it's so easy to become selfish.

—J. Stoll

Widows and Widowers

A Note to Family and Friends

First of all, a few words of appreciation for the care you have given me during the past months. Lying here in bed, unable to do much more than think, I realize it must take much patience on your part to leave your families for your turn on duty here for a day and a night. It was not by choice that I have been a helpless bed patient. My wish would have been to follow my wife when she died peacefully after only a brief illness. But God has a purpose in this, even though it is hidden from us. It may be a test of our faith.

I feel thankful that my family and neighbors have enough concern to care for me here at home. It would be heartbreaking to have to live out these last days in an old people's home. Those have their places, too, but one hopes the Plain churches may hold what they have kept through the years and continue to give tender loving care at home to their aged. If at times the way seems hard, just remember that someday you, too, may have a disability, and then you will appreciate the care you receive from the next generation.

Surely if your labor is done in a loving spirit, you shall not be unrewarded. And the King shall say unto them, "Verily, I say unto you, Inasmuch as you have done it unto one of the least of these my brethren, you have done it unto me" [Matthew 25:40].

—Your Aged Father

This Lonely Road

Since I have been a widow, I have become aware of how little thought or regard is given to the widow, and this probably holds true for the singles too. I do not want to leave the impression that no one in our church does anything for the widow. There are some who do plenty and regret that they can't do more, but the majority are like myself before I walked this lonely road. They have their own troubles and their own work to do, and don't bother to think of others as they should.

—A Widow from the East

Widowhood—a Life of Loneliness

In many larger communities, there are many widows and numerous activities for them. Widows' quiltings and comforter knottings are not uncommon. Widows are often invited to other people's homes for meals. There they meet others who, like themselves, have outlived their companions. They can share their trials and problems with each other, and give each other encouragement. These gatherings serve a worthwhile purpose, as long as they are not overdone.

Ask any widow who has experienced it, however, and she will tell you that being invited to eat with a family does not bring the satisfaction that being invited to *help* does. With all the help we neighbors can give the widows around us, their lives still contain moments of loneliness, of sighing, of tribulation, and of grief. It is certainly our duty to do what we can to lighten their burden as much as possible by helping them, praying for them, visiting them, and doing what we can to make them feel like useful and needed members of our society.

—Anonymous

In-Laws

Living with In-Laws

People who live with in-laws can perhaps be classed in three categories:

- Those who say it is impossible to live in peace with in-laws.

- Those who say it can be done with sincere effort.

- Those who find it a joy to share a farm with their partner's parents.

Most of the people who wrote us fit in the second category, those who feel it is possible, but it takes effort on both sides.

When we stop and think about the people who don't get along with their in-laws, and don't make any effort to keep it a secret that they don't, we often realize that the problem doesn't stop there. When they get done telling you about the faults of their in-laws, they will start complaining about other people— the neighbors, the ministers, the schoolteacher, sometimes even their own husbands.

Over the years they apparently have trained themselves so well to look for other people's faults that they can't help but see them [and mull over them]. I feel sorry for people like that. Think of the many friends they fail to enjoy.

When I hear a young woman talk about her mother-in-law, I can't help but think ahead. In a few short years, she will probably have some married sons. Then she will be in the mother-in-law's shoes. Will she be able to get along with her daughters-in-law? Human nature does not seem to improve over the generations. Unless she comes to realize that the biggest problem is within herself, she has little chance of getting along with her future daughters-in-law, or with anyone else, for that matter.

—Anonymous

Alone in the House

Once upon a time our house was filled with tears and laughter, quarrels and noisy play, the patter of little feet as in and out they went, the lisping of a baby making some first words. When washday came, it was a pleasure to whisk those dirty clothes into the washing machine and watch the clean things come out. The wash line was then filled, and oftentimes the fence beside it too.

When mealtime came, the table was stretched out long and filled with simple foods. What a pleasure to watch it disappear! With hearty appetites, it took a lot of cooking and baking.

On school days after four o'clock, we'd listen for the sound of feet marching across the porch. On wintry days they would be stomping and sweeping snow off boots before they'd all file in.

There was always a lot of sewing and also the altering of passed-down things. Every time I did it, I would have to marvel at the length of each new dress. The children were growing so fast.

In our family, grandparents also had their place. They took care of themselves and their rooms for many years. Through the busy summer months, they'd come and help us slice pears and apples, clean the beans and berries, and shell the peas. What a time we had, sitting on the porch, grandparents, half a dozen children, the hired girls, and myself, each with a dish of peas. Sometimes while working we would sing or play some thinking game.

Now the grandparents are gone. They are laid to rest in the graveyard yonder. Their house is empty. Nothing remains with us but memories. Some are very dear to the heart, but there are also memories of sickness and suffering, patience, and many lonely hours. Did we appreciate them enough while we had them? Those are the thoughts that come to me as I walk through the empty rooms, my footsteps echoing and reechoing.

Only now do I realize how good it was to have the house so full of people, even if I was knee-deep in work. Now I often think of those homes where there are young folks and old folks who are hoping and dreaming of better days to come. Please let me remind you that all too soon those children will grow up and be gone, and the old folks will be laid to rest. Then you may find yourself in a quiet and orderly home—yes, but in a lonely one.

I know. I too have yearned for those things, and now I have them. But something far more precious is gone, and for me never more to return. Now I am all alone in the house.

—Anonymous

Illness and Death

Family Life has printed many moving letters and articles by those who lost loved ones to illness or accident. Here are a few:

Our Time of Testing

[From a mother whose sixteen-month-old daughter, Naomi, recovered from an illness.]

Many thoughts raced through our minds as we sat by her bedside. We would rather see her die peacefully than to continue suffering as she was. We knew little children were promised the kingdom of heaven. We would sooner see her called home now than to grow up, fall into sin, and be lost forever. But I hope we will not forget the lesson we had needed so badly—to be able to give ourselves up and pray, "Thy will be done."

—Mrs. Eli E. Miller Jr.

Why

[From a mother whose baby died soon after birth.]

Of course, all the time the question "Why?" comes to our minds. But we should not expect to be able to understand everything in this life, and should never put a question mark where God has put a period.

—Ontario mother

A Memoriam for a Child Who Died of Cerebral Palsy

LaMar Lynn Diener at five years old,
Left this world to join God's fold.
He was one of God's chosen few—
Temptation to evil he never knew.

He left this earth in heaven to sing,
The rest of us closer to Jesus to bring.
Though parents and sisters miss him so—
We're glad for LaMar that he could go.

—Jake Diener

Who'll Be Next?

"Did you hear that Aaron Riehl drowned?"

"Aaron Riehl?" I said with a shocked tone.

"Yes, on Sunday evening. He and some of the other boys were swimming, and he drowned."

Next morning we walked across the field to the Riehls, since Aaron was single and at home yet. Neighbors were cleaning out the barn for the funeral service. Inside, women were helping too. Mrs. Riehl greeted us and also the rest of the family that was there. "Do you want to see Aaron?" she asked.

"Yes," I replied. They took us into the next room, where he lay. To me it looked like he was sleeping, so healthy and strong he looked. I thought I should say something to comfort the brokenhearted mother. But it seemed I couldn't say anything. Since the funeral was the next day, I helped a little to get ready.

The next day I was over to help with the horses, and then went up to the barn for the funeral. Two ministers preached. Sometimes they wept a little, and it seemed to me like a touching service. After a prayer, we viewed the body, and then he was carried to the graveyard.

There the coffin was opened for the final time. After we filed past again, the family gathered to look upon his face for the last time. Something like that is very touching, and I can't see how one can keep from shedding tears. I watched while they looked and wept. Then he was let down into the newly dug grave and covered with fresh earth. I had to wonder how the family felt, as it seemed to rend my heart.

Just recently I stopped at the graveyard and walked to look where he lay. It wondered me: If he could come back and talk to me, what he would say? Would he tell me to lead a more concerned and Christian life? Would he tell me not to think so much of the worry and cares of the world? Would he tell me to think more of the hereafter, of things above and not of things below?

But isn't that what he did tell us by leaving us so suddenly? Wasn't it to get me to think on things like that? But alas, how soon that is forgotten. Who'll be next—the next one to remind me?

—David W. Oberholtzer

TWELVE

Controversies

IT SHOULD COME AS NO SURPRISE to the reader by now that not all the Amish agree on everything. Indeed, the variety and differences in Amish lifestyle and religious interpretation across North America is surprising. The spectrum runs the gamut, from conservative to liberal, yet all within the scope of the Old Order faith. Naturally, the pages of *Family Life* can be a forum where these different views, opinions, and perspectives may be aired, even if agreement remains elusive.

Changing situations in the modern world often bring on these debates, and such is the case with insurance of different kinds. Some Amish accept liability insurance, but most do not accept commercial life, accident, or health insurance. Thus, the problem of paying large medical bills resulted in the idea of an Amish Aid Plan, as well as other internal plans that some communities now have. Many saw this as a way for church members to help each other, rather than being "unequally yoked" (2 Corinthians 6:14) to an outside, worldly insurance company. Others saw it as insurance in just another form.

Insurance

What about the Aid Plan?

With medical and hospital bills rising steadily over the years, some of our people feel that something should be done to ease this financial burden. I believe it is out of good intentions that some of our people are advocating an Amish Aid Plan. Although it may seem like a good plan, we want to be careful that we do not turn away from what the Bible teaches us: "Trust in the Lord with all your heart, and lean not upon your own understanding" (Proverbs 3:5).

Some people feel that the alms are not always used where most needed, but that under the new plan, this will be taken care of. This may be true, but if I understand the aid plan, then it will enable the well-to-do man to collect the same as the poorer man.

The Bible teaches us to give alms and aid the needy, but nowhere can I find that it teaches to help those that don't need it. In Proverbs 22:16, Solomon says, "He that oppresses the poor to increase his riches, and he that gives to the rich, shall surely come to want."

Some people say that the aid plan will help to do away with our people having hospitalization. It may not be as bad as being involved in a worldly company, but yet if it is not scriptural, it cannot be justified.

In the sixth chapter of Matthew, Jesus teaches us how to give alms. If done in secret, our heavenly Father will reward us openly. Under the aid plan, the need to give alms will be lessened. Since each person is expected to pay the same and anyone can collect, we can hardly expect a blessing to be in store for us.

Perhaps at times some of our people think they are not being helped as they should be, but maybe it is God's way of teaching patience.

Suppose God would let everything be taken away from us. I'm afraid any kind of insurance would fail us then. If God would let something like that befall us, it might help us to see our need of putting our complete trust in him. "Humble yourselves therefore under the mighty hand of God, that he may exalt you in due time; casting all your care upon him, for he cares for you" (1 Peter 5:6-7).

—I. B.

In Whom Do We Trust: God or Insurance?

Many people are telling us it is no longer safe to live without insurance of some kind. Are we afraid that we will be sued? Do we have insurance to protect us from this? If we do, how is that consistent with what Jesus said: "If any man sue you at the law and take away your coat, let him have your cloak also" (Matthew 5:40)?

But you say times have changed. You say that today the worldly people are merciless and would sue for more than is right, making it dangerous to be on the road [with a horse and buggy].

We agree that times have indeed changed. Four hundred years ago it was even dangerous for God's people to stay at home. Our forebears were inhumanely treated in many ways: their bodies stretched on the rack, their legs broken, their fingers cut off, and their tongues burned out. They were buried alive, roasted, stoned, crucified, drowned, beheaded, left in the cold to freeze, had molten lead poured down their throats, and were left in filthy dungeons for years with no companions but the vermin. Yes, times have changed.

Our forebears had no insurance except the protection of God. But today we think we have to have insurance because "it isn't safe to go on the roads." We cannot deny that times have changed, but which time would we rather have lived in?

Man wants to do things the human way. He wants to be his own savior. Or he relies on his good works for salvation. All this is trusting in man rather than exercising faith in God.

In today's world, insurance policies are taken for granted as a part of life. This is not surprising, for the world does not have faith and does not trust God. They do not have the living God of heaven and earth to rely on for their protection. They do not believe that God will do what he says in the Bible.

Is insurance then limited to nonreligious people? Sadly, the answer is no. Protestants and Catholics alike consider it no sin to protect their belongings, and even their lives, through insurance. The people of this world insure themselves in large companies for protection against loss of property. This may be all right for those who do not know God. But God promises in his Word that he will care for his children, in his own way; the world naturally does not believe this.

Nowadays, people say they are afraid they will be sued for all they are worth. They don't want to lose all that they have worked so hard to get. It's too dangerous to be without insurance. Yes, times have changed! But God is the same.

—Monroe D. Hochstetler

Tourism

Not for Sale

The women in our area are so busy making things for the tourist trade. Yes, it gives them extra money to spend. Of course, even the men are busy. "It pays better than farming," some are saying. Things are being made to cash in on the tourist trade that we would not approve of having ourselves, such as a lot of lawn ornaments and decorations.

Should we not try to make our living by growing or building something that is useful to mankind? Is it any wonder our

roads are heavy with the tourists when our own people are joining in to attract them? Some young women don't even have
time to sew for their families. What is happening to us?

A Quilting Mother

In our area there is a great demand for handmade quilts. There
are several younger and older women who spend some time
in the long winter hours to make some quilts to sell. Most of
us are not so well-to-do, and every available income is used to
help along with average family expenses.

Often the quilt money is needed promptly to help make one
payment or another. My husband is grateful to me whenever I
sign that quilt check and hand it to him. (He fully supports me
in my quilting hobby.) As I think of the hours I labored and the
fingers I pricked until they bled, I feel it is a great reward when
the quilt is sold and another debt can be paid.

It is not an unusual scene in our home in the winter months
to find me engrossed at one side of a quilt, with my preschool
youngsters seated on a bench on the other side, eyes sparkling,
their faces lit up with bright smiles, eagerly waiting for their
mother to begin to tell stories—Bible stories, stories of her
childhood, or to teach them to count or play games involving
colors and numbers.

In the summer months, you will find me in the fields, labor-
ing at my husband's side, struggling to keep up with the housework, childcare, canning, and all the numerous jobs the average
mother and housewife must attend to.

Profiting from the Amish Label

Do we stand alone? What do others think about using the
Amish name to make money, such as advertising "Amish
quilts," or "Amish girl wants housework," or "We serve dinners

in our Amish home"? Is there any wonder some settlements are overrun by tourists? What do others think about this? I would like to know.

Misusing the Amish Name

No, you do not stand alone. We also feel it is wrong to use the Amish name to sell something. Here in Lancaster County, the tourist bureau and many local businesses advertise [while] using the Amish name to increase their trade. This is bad enough without us ourselves doing it. Our Anabaptist fore-fathers suffered persecution for their faith. Nowadays the Amish name is being exalted far too much, and I don't believe it is for our good. Even if we feel we are selling an exceptional product, God, who gave us our talents, should be given all the glory. I feel also that it is wrong to make or sell Amish dolls to shops and stores that are frequented by tourists. We do not dress the way we do just to put on a show, so why should we put dolls out for the tourist public? May we strive to be a more humble people.

Tourists May Strengthen Our Faith

Coming in contact with tourists every day may have a detri-mental effect on some of our people, but there is another effect on many of us. Over and over they tell us we have something worth keeping. This has a strengthening effect on us.

—R. J. Y.

Giving an Answer for Our Hope

There is a difference between the tourist who is out seeking sights and the traveler who is genuinely interested in the beliefs of a religious group. The latter type deserves our attention and a fair answer.

The idea of being viewed like some specimen on display in a museum is not exactly to our liking. Also, being in the spotlight of the public eye is an undesirable situation.

It does seem strange that we, as Amish people, are suddenly objects of great interest to many people. This is such a contrast to the times of our Anabaptist forebears, who were ridiculed and persecuted as an unwanted people. Now, as the world struggles under the pressure and tension of modern living, there is much interest in us. For some, the interest goes deeper than just our lifestyle, for they can see that it is only a part of our precious faith. We certainly have the responsibility to give such people an answer for "the hope within us" [1 Peter 3:15].

—Cephas Kauffman

THIRTEEN

People of Peace

AS DESCRIBED AT THE BEGINNING of this book, the early Anabaptists suffered torture and death for their beliefs, yet met their fate with quiet resignation. They resisted with words but not with physical violence. They showed their faith and changed other people's lives by their examples, not by force. This heritage of nonresistance continues and has put some of the Amish to their most severe personal tests in the twentieth and twenty-first centuries.

We read the horrible stories of intolerance from hundreds of years ago and feel that we are so much more "civilized" today. Yet it is sobering to be reminded that humanity's greatest atrocities toward their fellow humans occurred just a few decades ago, in our own lifetime.

The Revolutionary War, the Civil War, World Wars I and II, the Vietnam War—these violent times created challenges for Amish, Mennonites, and others who believe in nonviolence and Jesus' call to love the enemy. Those who refuse to take up arms to defend their country are often viewed with suspicion, even hatred.

These stories are a lesson in how societies respond to those who are "different," and in the power of faith during adversity. Regardless of what your personal feelings may be in these matters, you will come away pondering the issue of religious freedom in an increasingly violent and intolerant world.

The Revolutionary War

In 1776, when the American colonies declared their independence from England, all the colonists were expected to help fight the English. Naturally, the Amish, being nonresistant, refused to do this. Because they refused to be drafted into the army, some Berks County [Pa.] Amishmen were arrested. These men were placed in prison. After a speedy trial, the Amish prisoners were sentenced to death and the date of execution was set.

The death penalty, however, was never put into effect. A minister in the local German Reformed church pleaded with the authorities to release the Amish prisoners. He said they had fled Europe to avoid military service and that they shouldn't be expected to do in America what their consciences had told them was wrong in Europe. He also testified that the Amish are quiet and unassuming people, doing harm to no one. Because of his testimony, the government freed the men, but not without fining them and making them pay a tax for hiring a substitute.

Amish Settlers and the Civil War

It was the time of the Civil War, in the land bordering the Mason-Dixon Line and the western tip of Maryland. Daniel Beachy, the Amish bishop in that region, and his people had heard rumors of the war in the East and South, and they knew the danger of being caught in destructive border skirmishes.

A quiet and peace-loving people, Daniel and his followers prepared for such an emergency, not by loading their muskets, but by planning escape routes for their families and hideouts for the livestock. Daniel's wife, Elizabeth, packed a set of clothing for each of their eight children in a bedsheet, which she planned to hide in a nearby cave if the need arose. This took more than a trip to town to buy extra clothing. It meant countless hours of spinning, weaving, knitting, and sewing by hand.

It turned out that no actual battles were fought in their part of the Alleghenies, near the village of Aurora, West Virginia. But to the north of them lay the B&O Railroad, coveted by the Confederates. And through their area passed the main turnpike (now U.S. 50), also a prized possession.

Daniel Beachy realized early in the war that this land could well become an easy target for the Confederate raiders. As bishop of the Gortner-Aurora congregation, he went about encouraging his flock to put their trust in God, but not to ignore any warnings that might reach them.

From their farm nestled in a valley just northwest of Aurora, the Beachys saw many troops of both Union and Confederate soldiers, marching on the turnpike. In fact, one troop of Union soldiers, apparently stationed to guard the pike, camped for several weeks on the Beachy farm. Although they were of a friendly nature, the soldiers did take some of the Beachys' supplies. When the troops left, the young Beachys swarmed the campsite and enjoyed some hardtack candy the soldiers left behind.

The time passed peacefully for the Amish until Crist Petersheim, a neighbor of the Beachys and a member of his church, was captured by the graycoats (Southerners). Mrs. Petersheim, having no clue as to what had become of her husband, spent a week of anxiety alone with six small children.

After forcing Mr. Petersheim to haul supplies for them with his team and wagon for a week, the soldiers permitted him to return to his home.

To add to this, in March 1863 the federal Conscription Act [also known as the Enrollment Act] was passed; it made no provision for conscientious objectors. News of this law reached into the larger Amish settlement in northern Garrett County, Maryland, and Somerset County, Pennsylvania. The law did permit, however, the hiring of substitutes or the payment of a $300 tax instead of subscription [signing up to serve in the army].

How did the Amish respond to this law? Records show that the Amish Mennonite churches of Garrett and Somerset Counties raised a sum of $16,000 to pay the taxes of their drafted members. Apparently, drafted men reported personally to headquarters and paid these dues. But this was all a part of the wartime, and they took it in stride.

Despite impending dangers, the Gortner-Aurora Amish continued to hold church services every two weeks in their scattered homes. Always aware of the danger of being captured, Bishop Beachy regularly made the long trips about this community by horseback to minister to his flock.

Then came the raid led by General William Jones in the spring of 1863. Jones's primary purpose was to destroy the bridges on the turnpike and cripple the B&O Railroad. His second objective was to collect horses, cattle, and supplies. He was forced to do this by the sea blockade, which had caused a serious shortage of many items in the South. Wild inflation made the price of a pair of shoes soar to $400, and a barrel of flour sold for $1,000.

Unlike the destructive raid that General Sheridan led into the South, General Jones's orders were to seize cattle, horses, and supplies indiscriminately, but to respect other private property at all times. So the Amish escaped the destructive loss that some communities suffered.

On April 26, 1863, a beautiful Sunday morning after days of heavy rains, Daniel Beachy mounted his dainty mare, Baldy, and set out for Gortner to preach at the Joseph Slabach farm. Riding along the turnpike, he was joined by two of his members, Crist Petersheim and Peter Schrock. As the three men traveled eastward, they met Confederate soldiers straggling along the muddy road. Approaching the Maryland state line from the west, they rode squarely into the main force of General Jones's army.

The men drew their horses up on the road bank to let the soldiers pass. But a trooper, evidently in a jovial mood, approached Mr. Beachy, jerked off his hat, and clapped his own officer's cap on him. At the same time, he put Beachy's broad-brimmed hat on his own head. After a round of loud guffaws about the joke, he again changed hats as well as his manner, gruffly demanding that Mr. Beachy dismount and give up his horse.

Daniel remained calmly seated. His blue eyes were fearless as he replied, "Sir, I cannot give up my horse. I need it for farming."

The trooper stared in disbelief at this man who refused to obey his orders. Clearing his throat, he said roughly, "Sir, if you don't get off that horse, I'll put you off." Profanity rattled about like hailstones as the trooper began to unbuckle the saddle girths.

Still Mr. Beachy remained seated. Crist Petersheim spoke up: "Sir, we are on our way to church, and this man is our preacher. How shall he get there if you take his horse?"

Instantly, the trooper stopped, glancing about uneasily for the officer in command. "Why didn't you tell me sooner?" Quickly rebuckling the saddle girths, he sent the men on their way.

Urging their horses into a brisk trot, they hastened on to the Maryland state line and turned north on the Oakland road, which was clear. Arriving at the Slabach farm, Daniel Beachy and a fellow minister held a short church and prayer service.

After church they learned that Colonel Harmon, with a detachment of a thousand men, had captured the Union troops on guard at Oakland and had invaded the town. The soldiers were now destroying bridges, crippling the railroad, and scouring the countryside for cattle, horses, and supplies.

Men hurriedly drove their cattle and horses into hiding. Daniel Beachy and his companions retreated to a deep woods and stayed under cover until dusk, when they set out through the forest for their homes. They forded treacherous streams swollen by heavy rains. Finally, Daniel tied his horse in the forest near his home and walked home, carrying the heavy saddle.

Meanwhile, Elizabeth Beachy, at home with her eight children, was alarmed at the sight of hundreds of soldiers carrying the Confederate flag, marching westward on the turnpike. But where was her husband? Quickly she went to the loft and got several pieces of cured meat. Taking them out in front of the house, she dropped them into a hole between some rocks and covered them with sticks and stones. Then she instructed her two older sons, ten and thirteen years old, to drive the cattle and horses back of the barn, beyond the lime quarry and into the forest. They left only one old horse in the stable.

While the soldiers stopped in Aurora to raid David Ridenhour's store of everything eatable or wearable, the boys made a fast getaway with the livestock. Mother Beachy's alarm grew as a group of the men in gray turned in at the Beachy lane. Horrible stories about Confederate raids raced through her mind. With frightened children clinging to her skirts, she clasped baby Lena to her breast and watched them approach.

But the men went past the little one-room log house and rode on to the stable.

The soldiers wanted cattle and horses and forage for their horses. They fed their horses and left, taking the Beachys' old horse and leaving a worn-out horse in its stead. Three times during the day, small groups of soldiers came in to the farm to feed their horses, each time exchanging a worn-out horse for the one that had rested in the stable. The horse that they left there at last was worthless.

As the long afternoon wore on and Daniel did not return, Elizabeth Beachy became more uneasy. At twilight, when the coast was clear of soldiers, she slipped back to the forest with the boys to help milk the cows. [Much later, after the family was in bed, Daniel finally arrived home.]

Even after these episodes, the little Amish colony refused to be dismayed. Bishop Daniel Beachy continued to lead his flock in love and unity. Every two weeks they gathered to hear his admonitions.

Although lines of anxiety did show in Elizabeth Beachy's kindly face, her hands were never idle. Despite her many duties, she found time to be neighborly. Committing herself into God's care, she walked miles to carry a nourishing dish or offer a helping hand to a sick neighbor.

Besides the anxiety of war, there were the family crises that they went through together. Unaided by a doctor, Daniel and Elizabeth ushered three new babies into their home during this time. And their three-month-old Susie had been laid to rest beside her little brother in the graveyard on the hillside.

Undoubtedly, the Beachys rejoiced when the end of the war was announced. No longer would Father need to be on the lookout for raiders as he went about his work. No longer would Mother need to defy danger to make her neighborly calls.

Today, as one drives through the settlement at Gortner, there are no scars to show what took place there a century ago. Old Backbone Mountain is mute to what happened here in his shadow. But the Amish descendants tell us these fragments of the past.

—Mary Elizabeth Yoder

World War I and the Arrest of an Amish Bishop

The United States entered World War I on April 6, 1917, and had as its main opponent Germany. To support its war efforts, the U.S. government issued a series of five war bonds known as Liberty or Victory bonds. These were not taxes but requests by the government that American citizens loan money to help wage the war. The buyer of a bond received anywhere from 3.5 to 4.75 percent interest. The American people loaned their government nearly $21 billion by purchasing war bonds.

Since purchasing war bonds was to be voluntary, the Amish, Mennonites, and other nonresistant Americans should not have been affected. But the bonds were voluntary in name only. Each community was assigned a quota and had a committee of local citizens to see that the quota was reached. This meant that the local people put pressure on their fellow citizens to buy war bonds. It was a classic example of high-pressure salesmanship. Anyone who hesitated to buy a war bond was labeled a "second-class citizen," "traitor," or "friend of the enemy."

Since the war was being waged with Germany, all American citizens of German background were naturally suspected by their neighbors as being possible traitors. One way to test them was to ask them to buy war bonds. This anti-German sentiment was felt by all Americans of German descent. Since the Amish and Mennonites were "Germans" too, in the public's opinion, they felt the pressure quite a bit. But the pressure differed from area to area.

[These are the accounts of] Amishmen who remember what the pressure was like at the time the war bonds were being urged upon all Americans:

War Bonds in Lancaster County, Pennsylvania

The first airplanes I ever saw in flight passed over us in the fall of 1918. They were dropping leaflets urging purchase of bonds. I did not hear of much pressure but heard several ministers, one a bishop, had been somehow pressured to buy, but were able to back out again. It seems we here in Lancaster County have had lenient draft boards and a good feeling between us and "outsiders."

War Bonds in Reno County, Kansas

Yes, I remember well of some of the pressure and also the hard feeling it gave at that time. I was a young man and was just ordained to the ministry a year before. Of course, they thought I just took up the ministry to get exempted from the draft, and said I had to get an affidavit to show I was ordained by lot. Then, since my dad was bishop, he made up a writing and got a few signatures, so that settled that.

They then came and said every member over twenty-one has to buy a war or Liberty bond. The Amish didn't want to buy any because we felt it would be helping the war. Well, we had a real nice banker here in our little town of Yoder. He helped us all he could. So our people, just to try to keep peace, went and bought bonds and gave them to the banker as a present and never asked for the money back.

Since we were married a few years, we were very hard up at the time. But there was no other way. So we had to borrow seventy-five dollars to buy a bond. So we just did like most of the others. But I remember a few older men who refused to buy any. One day some officers came to Noah Beachey's, knocked at the door, and asked Mrs. Beachy where Mr. Beachy was. She said she didn't know where he was. But they didn't believe her and opened the door and went in and hunted in every room, in closets, under beds, and everywhere.

Mr. Beachy had seen them come and had hidden outside somewhere. So when they couldn't find him, they told Mrs. Beachy that if he didn't buy a bond by such a time, they would tar and feather him. They were in much fear for a few days and then went and bought one.

Then the officers went over to Mr. Kaufman. They warned him the same way, then also went to a Mr. Bontrager. So I think after it was all over with, everybody did the same and just turned the bonds over to the banker.

Conscientious Objection to War

War bonds were a new type of test for the Amish churches. Should they or could they in conscience purchase the bonds? The ministers felt their members should not purchase any, for by doing so they would be helping to wage the war. But some churches, such as the Reno County (Kans.) church, experienced such pressure that they reluctantly purchased bonds, but refused to accept them back after the war was over. To some people this seemed a solution, and to others a compromise. Those who felt it was wrong to purchase bonds, even under severe pressure, compared the situation to that of Amish boys who were being drafted.

The United States made few provisions for conscientious objectors when war was declared on April 6, 1917. The only provision was that they must go to the army and wear the uniform, but could perform noncombatant work. So the Amish boys were drafted, sent to the army camps, and expected by their home churches to remain steadfast under mockery, persecution, and severe pressure. But now back home, members were going partway and reluctantly purchasing the war bonds. This went down hard with many Amish people, for they wondered how their boys could be expected to bear the test in the army camps if they heard that the people back home were compromising.

With such thoughts in mind, one person decided something should be said about the situation. Manasses E. Bontrager, bishop of the now extinct Amish church at Dodge City, Kansas, put his letter [which contained his thoughts on bonds and conscientious objectors] in an envelope, sealed and stamped it, and mailed it to *The Budget* office in Ohio, which printed it for May 15, 1918.

Several months passed. A U.S. marshal arrived at the peaceful Kansas farm of fifty-year-old Manasses Bontrager and arrested him. The marshal said that Bontrager had written a letter to an Ohio newspaper. Part of the letter was in violation of Section 3, Title I, Espionage Act of June 15, 1917. He along with *The Budget* editor, S. H. Miller, would have to appear before a judge in federal court in Cleveland, Ohio, the federal district in which *The Budget* was published.

Manasses's second son remembers when the marshal took his father away: "The way I remember it, the U.S. officer treated father with all consideration possible. He did not mistreat Father or use any harsh words. When they went to the depot in Dodge City, he bought a ticket and gave it to Father so that nobody on the train could know he was under arrest. I think Father stayed in a hotel room while in Cleveland."

On August 5, the trial of Manasses Bontrager and S. H. Miller was held. [The following excerpts are from] an account of the trial as reported on page 1 of Cleveland's largest newspaper, *The Plain Dealer*, on August 6, 1918:

> Federal Judge Westenhaver yesterday imposed a fine of $500 on Rev. Manasses E. Bontrager of Dodge City, Kansas, a bishop in the Amish Mennonite church, after Bontrager had entered a plea of guilty to violation of the espionage act. . . .
>
> "When the country is at war," Judge Westenhaver told the bishop, "you and all who benefit by its powers are equally bound to bear the burden. Religious liberty such as you enjoy was not gained by nonresistance. No persons in this country regret the war more than those not of your faith.
>
> "No man, no matter how rich he may be, can buy exemption; no man may furnish a substitute. But out of consideration for your religious belief, there has been granted to your young men exemption from combatant service."
>
> The bishop announced in court that he would henceforth leave the matter of bond buying and military service to the individual consciences of members of his church.
>
> "I made a mistake by writing that letter," he confessed. "I did wrong. I thank Mr. Kavanagh and the judge for showing me my error."
>
> As an individual, Bishop Bontrager declared he was "still opposed to killing Germans."
>
> "But I want Germany beaten," he added. "I shall pray that they may be. Perhaps the Lord will destroy them as he destroyed the Egyptians."

Manasses Bontrager paid his $500 fine immediately and returned to Kansas. He had received offers from prominent people in Dodge City to help pay his fine, but he paid it himself.

How could a person be fined for advising others not to buy something that wasn't legally required of them in the first place? The newspapers do not supply us with the real reason for his arrest and fining. The answer is found in File No. 186400-18 at the Department of Justice in Washington, D.C.

In one letter the U.S. attorney general asked the U.S. attorney of the federal district of Cleveland to explain why Bontrager and Miller were fined. In his letter of response, the Cleveland U.S. attorney made no mention of war bonds. He gave the reason for their arrest and fining as "for inciting and attempting to incite subordination, disloyalty, and refusal of duty in the military and naval forces of the United States." Bontrager had written, "What would become of our nonresistant faith if our young brethren in camp would yield?" The government considered this sentence as encouraging COs not to obey the commands of their army officers to perform military duty. Such an attitude and statement, the Cleveland U.S. attorney pointed out, was in violation of the 1917 Espionage Act.

The event is now a part of Amish history. We need not take pride in it but should not feel shame either. An Amish bishop unknowingly wrote a letter in a public paper [advocating what] was not legally supposed to be done. But morally he was not guilty. In fact, his letter undoubtedly was a good moral influence on the lives of many people who saw it in *The Budget* in 1918. Who knows but that it may have helped many readers not to compromise their consciences.

—D. Luthy

Amish Army Camp Experiences

Excerpts from one of four accounts by Amish of their experiences as conscientious objectors in World War I army camps:

Camp Taylor, Kentucky
One day we were taken to a room where the bunk beds were set up. We were told to pile them up in a neat stack. When we

had finished, we were ordered to put them back again like they were. This kept on for quite some time.

On Sunday I was given some work, and when I refused, I was sent to the guardhouse. One of the guards became angry and struck me across the breast with the bayonet of his gun, nearly knocking me down. The same guard also struck one of the Ohio boys, knocking him down and stabbing him with his bayonet. He made a cut in his pants and a gash in his hip about two inches long.

On July 11, we were released from the guardhouse and sent back to our company, where we met more trials. We were taken to the latrine and given orders that it must be cleaned. But we refused to obey the orders, so the commander got a broomstick and beat me across the legs till he broke his stick. I had streaks and swellings on my legs. Then we were taken back to the orderly room and told that we would be tried by a special board of inquiry, and if we were found sincere, we could be let out on farm furlough.

But our trials started again, and July 28 was one of my hardest days. It was a Sunday, and they were determined that we must work. They ordered us to pick up all the cigarette stubs that lay on the parking lot grounds, and when we refused, we were thrown on the ground. We were kicked and knocked around, and finally I was taken to a building where the company commander said he would teach me to fight. He began hitting me in the face with his hands until I began going down. Then he would quit for a moment. Another fellow helped him, and they kept on till I started to fall, and one of the men would catch me so I would not fall down.

Finally, one of my partners and I were ordered to carry a can of sweepings, which we did. Then we were taken around to see what was done to the other partner. He was out on the public road with his face and head well marked with blue bumps and marks, and a sign hanging on him that read, "I refuse to fight for my country." Then we were sent back to our barracks.

The next morning the first lieutenant asked us, "Are you now willing to wear uniforms?"

When we said we weren't, he had the government overalls taken off us, which we were wearing, and said we should wear the clothes that God gave us. We were compelled to stand naked till noon the next day.

On August 10, the major of the camp heard of how we were being used. We were called upon to witness in a court-martial against our officers.

About September 6, we were again called upon to witness, and when we refused, we were put under guard. The reason the officials were court-martialed was for disobeying military law in striking anyone on the camp grounds. We felt that we could not conscientiously testify against them, for it would be helping to punish them.

On November 1, we met the special board of inquiry and were passed for farm furloughs.

—Menno A. Deiner

Before their release, one man's wife died. The war ended November 11, 1918. One Amishman reported abuse at another camp, such as being hung by the neck until unconscious. Another finished his letter about Fort Oglethorpe, Georgia, this way:

What a Blessing!
On January 23, 1919, I was given a green discharge paper that read: "This man is a conscientious objector and has done no military duty whatsoever. He has refused to wear a uniform and is not recommended for re-enlistment." What a blessing!

—Levi S. Yoder

World War II

Amish COs in CPS Camps

During the war years of 1941–1945, Amish boys and other conscientious objectors in the United States were not drafted into the army. Instead, they were assigned to jobs that were in the interest of the public good. The program under which they worked was called Civilian Public Service, or simply CPS. While soldiers were stationed at army camps, the COs lived at separate CPS camps.

Some of the 441 Amish boys who served in CPS were given employment at mental hospitals; some served as firefighters in the forests of the far West; some volunteered to become human "guinea pigs" at hospitals where tests were being made for the prevention of various diseases. Others worked in forestry projects or were involved in studying better farming methods and soil conservation.

Altogether, there were 138 CPS camps scattered across the United States. Not all of them had Amish, but many did. One unit, the Boonsboro Camp in Maryland, was made up entirely of Amish boys. But generally the camps contained boys from various religious backgrounds. Two camps with a high percentage of Amish COs were Grottoes and Luray in Virginia.

The Way of Love

[Based on a World War II incident, from *The Story of Amish in Civilian Public Service*, by Bishop Ira Nissley.]

The man's knuckles shone white as he gripped the razor blade and slashed wildly through the air around him.

The scene took place during World War II when many Amish young men were in CPS camps and hospitals. The man with the razor blade was a patient in a mental hospital where some Amish conscientious objectors were serving their time until the war ended. The regular attendant, who was not a CO, had come upon the patient, but had quickly backed away and locked the door behind him. Even with four or five strong men to help him wrestle the patient down, there would still be a chance of someone getting injured. Yet something had to be done.

"Get those Amish boys who just believe in love and peace," someone suggested, with a bit of mockery in his voice. "Let them handle him. This is a good job for them."

Three COs were called in and told to get the razor blade from the man. They sensed at once the importance of the test to which they were being put. The other attendants were watching them to see what they would do.

With a prayer in their hearts, the three consulted together for a few seconds. Then two of them sent off to get a mattress, and the third unlocked the door for them when they came. The mattress appeared to be more than they could handle in the narrow doorway. They heaved and fumbled and pulled. Finally, they looked up at the man [with the razor] and said, "Maybe you could give us a hand with this mattress?" The patient forgot all about his anger and violent intentions. He dropped the razor blade and grabbed the mattress. In that instant the third CO, with a flick of his hand, had the sharp blade and slipped out of the room and down the hall with it.

Everyone breathed easier. The battle had been won without violence. The regular attendants were surprised and a bit beaten out to see with what ease the COs had solved the problem.

Although cases might arise where it would not be wrong to wrestle a person to keep him from harming himself or others, these three COs were still far ahead to try to find a more peaceful solution. In so doing, they left a good example for the attendants watching them.

In the same way, in the problems and frustrations of our daily lives, we do well to seek peaceful means to settle disputes and difficulties. No matter how trifling or how great the problem, a solution based on gentleness, kindness, and love will surely prove to have been the better way in the end.

—E. Stoll

The Vietnam Years

Where to, I-W?

During the last year of World War I, many conscientious objectors found themselves in prison or army camps. Much has been written of their trials and sufferings. Most of the brethren proved steadfast in the faith and would have been willing to face the firing squad rather than go against their convictions.

As a result of this, provisions were made during the Second World War so that the COs did not need to go to the army camps. They were given work without pay, under civilian directions, something they could conscientiously do. The program was financed and operated by the churches. But when the war was over, the camps were closed. A few years later the draft was resumed, but the churches were not interested in going to the bother of opening more camps. It seemed much easier to turn the matter over to the government. This resulted in the I-W program of working in the hospitals.

"The Amish would never be able to operate their own camps," it has been said. Apparently many people have forgotten that the Amish did operate their own camp during World War II at Boonsboro, Maryland. The churches of Pennsylvania were responsible for this camp, and they did an excellent job. What about the need for a better place to send our I-W boys?

Behind Prison Walls

"In case of doubt, I feel it is best for Christians to choose the course that goes hardest against his nature or desires."

This bit of advice I heard when I was a boy. It was branded on my conscience. When I was called to report for I-W service, I decided it would indeed be easiest to go with the group. But my conscience would not allow it.

I was arrested for violating the Universal Military Service and Training Act. I was sentenced to prison for two years. But because my friends and customers (I am a blacksmith) interceded for me, my sentence was reduced to one year. My case received quite a bit of publicity over radio, on television, and by newspaper, which brought much sympathy from unknown friends in many states. But there were others who felt I should be dealt with more harshly.

On my arrival at the federal penitentiary in Lewisburg, Pennsylvania, one of my first trials was the barber chair. The barber, who was an inmate, was ordered to give me a shave and a haircut. Four officers stood by in case of trouble.

The barber explained to me several different styles of haircuts. Then he asked, "Which style do you prefer?"

"I do not want any other kind except the one I have," I answered.

He kept insisting that I pick one of the styles, but I steadfastly answered, "I will not choose any of the styles which you have to offer."

He sympathized with me and finally suggested that he could take off just enough to satisfy the officers. When he had finished, he put on enough grease so the hair would lay over in modern style. By the next morning my hair had returned to its normal position.

On the way to the mess hall, I was called aside and told to report to the barber shop again after breakfast. This time I was given a short crew cut, the style in which my hair was kept until I had served my time.

The first night I did not sleep very well. I dreamed that one of my younger brothers opened my cell door and came to stay with me so I would not be so lonesome. I thanked him, then begged him to go home because I did not feel it was a very nice place for such a young boy. I woke up with tears in my eyes. Now, four years later, this same brother is working out a two-year sentence on the same charge.

The next few days seemed long to me, alone in a cell without anything to read and no watch to see what time it was. Later they gave me my Testament.

From there I was transferred to an honor camp at Allenwood, Pennsylvania, where my job was shoeing horses and repairing gates, feed bunks, buildings, and so on. The second week some of us were called in and asked to volunteer to be moved to a new institution just finished by contractors. I told them I would rather not, and they said I wouldn't have to if I didn't want to. They couldn't get enough volunteers, so they placed about twenty of us on a list.

[The group was transported to a newly built prison in Marion, Illinois.] I was there only a few days till they demanded I change clothes. At the honor camp, my clothing was changed to make it a little more plain for me. But at the new place they refused to do so.

After a couple of days on an outside detail, I was called inside and locked in a five-by-seven-foot room with two of the biggest officers there. They ordered me to take off my clothes, which I did. Next they told me to put on the clean clothes. I refused to put them on. One of the officers hit me with the palm of his hand. Then they put [the clothes] on me. Then I went back to my job.

One time the inmates decided to take me to the movies. That evening some of the men came to persuade me to go along. I did not go, so the next time a group of them planned to take me by force. They claimed if I would go once, I would like it and would want to go again.

"You can lead an ox to the water, but you cannot make him drink," I told them.

They were going to take me anyway. A little before the time I expected them to pick me up, I decided I could take a shower. When they came, I was taking a shower, so they gave it up and didn't ask me to go any time later.

While I was in the gym one day, watching others play a game of shuffleboard, an inmate came over and slapped me across the face. It took me by surprise, and I didn't know why it was done. At once, the prisoner was ashamed of himself. We had always been friends. He told me some of them were betting that I would strike back, so they decided to test me. Actually, I was too much surprised to strike back. There were other times when they tried out my faith by betting with each other. It made me feel quite small.

I have been asked why I chose prison instead of serving in I-W. It was a hard decision to make, but I tried to go according to my understanding of the Scriptures.

Most of us are probably acquainted with Titus 3:1; 1 Peter 2:13; and Romans 13:1. "To be subject to the principalities and powers, to obey magistrates." "For there is no power but of God" But we are bound to obey only as long as it is in accordance with the Scriptures. In Matthew 5:39-44, Jesus says, "Whosoever shall smite you on your right cheek, turn to him the other also. . . . Love your enemies, bless them that curse you, do good to them that hate you, and pray for them which despitefully use you and persecute you."

The soldiers asked John the Baptist, "What shall we do?" and he said to them, "Do violence to no man" [Luke 3:14]. That leaves no room for war. If war is wrong in the eyes of God, how far can we go along with the law to register? I feel I could not sign my name on their papers again, although I did when I became eighteen years old.

When I refused to accept a job in the hospital, I received a sentence from a federal judge. The charges stated that I knowingly and willfully refused to report for the military service and training act. Had I reported, would I not have been a part of the military according to the act?

FOURTEEN

Odds and Ends

MY AMISH FRIENDS WOULD CERTAINLY take me to task if the reader came away from this collection thinking that the Amish are a pious, somber people who never laugh or have a good time. The pages of *Family Life* contain many delightful stories, most of which are drawn from personal observation and experiences. In them one can share both the humor and the joy of life's happier moments.

In this chapter you'll find a variety of odds and ends: humorous writing, home remedies, stories that fit the category "Believe it or not!" and poignant lessons about faith.

Ultimately, while going about their daily chores, Amish people find lessons for their own lives. In a sense, daily life and Christian faith come together here in the most natural way. Perhaps the stories in this chapter—humorous, ordinary, and faith-filled—best summarize "what it means to be Amish." They form a fitting conclusion to this book. Not unlike the parables in the Bible, these "Amish parables" from everyday life are meaningful for every one of us.

Out of the Mouths of Babes

I was teaching the children the Lord's Prayer, one line each evening at bedtime. One night I had to smother a laugh when our four-year-old volunteered, "Give us this day our jelly bread."

—E. K.

Around Christmastime last year, Daddy was reading to our three-year-old after breakfast one morning. He was reading the poem that tells about the shepherds bringing a lamb, the wise men bringing gifts, and so on. Then he came to the last two lines, "And what shall I give him? I'll give him my—"

Before he had a chance to say "Heart," our three-year-old said, "Oatmeal!"

—Mrs. R. L. Y.

"Why are you wiping the dust off the leaves of the rubber plant?" our three-year-old asked.

"So the plant can breathe," I answered.

The next morning the little girl energetically scrubbed the dirty washbowl. Surprised, I asked, "Why are you washing the washbowl?"

"So it can breathe," she answered.

—M. Z. M.

At the dinner table, our five-year-old began pouring his glass of water on his helping of fish. I asked him what he was doing, and he said he wanted to see if the fish would awake again.

Childish Ways

The Leaf Collection

My son had just started his leaf collection last spring, and spent hours in the woods collecting, labeling, and pressing them. The latter consisted of sticking them in old books, under newspapers, in drawers, and unknown to me, in our Bible and in our New Testament. Since we had an old Bible we used for everyday, I wasn't aware of this until the day church services were held at our house.

Our whole congregation was gathered in the shed. We had a very inspiring sermon by Uncle Mose from Northfield District. Then he gave a few final comments, glanced at the clock, and announced that it was time to read the text from the New Testament.

He picked up the book, opened it, and immediately a large oak leaf fell to the floor. A whimsical grin spread over his face, and as he turned the pages, some more leaves came fluttering down. I glanced up just in time to see a maple leaf land at Uncle Mose's feet. For a moment I couldn't believe my eyes, until I realized Johnny's leaf collection was being discovered. Uncle Mose regained his composure, found the correct text, and read the chapter while the stem of one leaf stuck out of the side of the book.

Bantam Rooster

Back when I was four or five,
(Or maybe I was six),
We had a bantam rooster
That got me in a fix.

When I was heading for the barn,
He'd stand and bar my way.
I guess he thought he owned that barn,
And all the cows and hay.
He's long been dead, with all his hens,
(And surely he had oodles).

I wonder how he met his end?
I hope he flavored noodles.

—Janice Etter

An Absentminded Husband

My husband's handicap is that he is absentminded, unbeliev-ably absentminded. He's constantly losing things.

He takes the flashlight to the barn, and it's never seen again. He uses a Vice-Grip wrench in the pigpen and leaves it lie to fetch a bolt from the shop. When he returns, the pigs have claimed the wrench and buried it in the manure.

In the house it's the same story. He starts a fire in the kitchen stove and leaves the plastic pail with corncobs on top of the stove.

At the table, the children and I have learned to expect any-thing when we ask Dad to pass a dish for us. The first problem is to get him to hear us. We often have to ask him three or four times to do a simple thing, like pass the bread. At last he will look up, truly sorry for having kept us waiting, and quickly pass the *milk*.

When our oldest daughter started going to school, she was so used to repeating everything she said that the teacher thought she stuttered.

Who wants to say things four times in the presence of company? One of the boys tried that one time. He sat right next to Dad, and so undertook to get his attention by tug-ging on his shirtsleeve. "You gave me too many beans. You gave me too many beans. You gave me too many beans." Finally, he did succeed in getting Dad's attention, but all that soaked in was the word *beans*. Dad smiled lovingly, nodded his head, and to the little boy's dismay, dished out some *more* beans!

Confession

When the absentminded husband in the story above found out how many people were condemning his wife for not being more loyal to him, it proved to be a time for confession. "I am horrified to know that people are criticizing my wife," he writes. "She is a patient, loving, kind person who has never done me a bad turn in her life. She does her best to look after me every waking hour. So in conclusion, let me say two things. The first thing—please don't blame my wife, for she didn't write that article at all. I wrote it *myself*, as it seemed to me the way my wife could feel many times. And the second thing—alas, I have forgotten what it was!"

Tourists

Typos

Mistakes do happen. Sometimes the result is humorous, sometimes startling and dangerous. Only one letter misplaced, or a word left out, can change the meaning.

One of the best examples of this we have ever seen appeared in the nationally distributed newspaper *Travel*. In the article "Ohio's Amish Country," there was supposed to be the statement "They do not bear arms, will not take *oaths*, and believe that the end of the world is imminent."

The typesetter got one letter wrong, and hundreds of readers learned a new fact about the Amish: "They will not take *baths*"!

So if you read something in a Pathway paper that you find hard to believe, check with us before you stop your subscription.

Local Entertainment

Isn't it true that all of us know what it feels like to do "something dumb"? Maybe that is why it makes us feel good every now and then to learn that others also make goofs. A while ago a reader in Lancaster County couldn't resist sending us two humorous incidents provided for the local residents by the area's tourists. Here is the first story as it was sent to us:

"This area is advertised across the United States as the place to go to see the Amish on the road and in the fields with horses. This spring a lady wanted to take a picture of an Amishman when he was plowing. She wanted him to stand next to her husband, beside his team of horses. The Amishman refused to do it, so she went to the state police office to report it. She wanted them to report him to his boss, or have him arrested, because she thought he was working for the state of Pennsylvania! She did not realize he was his own boss!

"The policeman on duty said he could hardly keep from laughing because she was so serious about this. He could not get her to understand that this is the way we live, and that we are not being paid by the state to farm and live the way we do so the tourists can come and watch us."

The next story was taken from a newspaper clipping entitled "Tourist Tells Shocking Story about Amish." The clipping predicted, "Local farmers will get a charge out of this story. A woman from New York was hoping to get some pictures of the Amish. She stopped by the side of the road, along with her son, and walked up to an electric fence [powered by a battery]. You can guess the rest. She reported the incident to the local chamber of commerce. Hopefully, the people there told her the fence was actually intended for straying livestock, and not straying tourists!"

Advice

Aggression Cookies

There are many ways to keep children out from underfoot on those rainy days or when you are busy. Older children can help you make Aggression Cookies.

3 cups oatmeal
1½ cup brown sugar
1½ cup flour
3 sticks [1½ cup] butter
1½ teaspoon baking powder

Let your children dump all the ingredients in a bowl. In this recipe, the fiercer the pounding, the better the cookies, so children can squeeze, mush, pound, pinch, slap, and hit the dough to their heart's content. Roll into small balls and bake on ungreased cookie sheet for 10 minutes at 350°F.

—Mrs. Andy Miller

For Sleep

If some nights sleep doesn't come, I don't count sheep; I talk to my Shepherd.

—Mrs. P. W. Jr.

Marking Clothing

A mother from Ontario has advised that instead of making children's stockings and other things with the child's initial, mark them with the child's age. When a garment is passed down, it will stay with the child nearest that age, and they will be able to find their belongings without confusion. This works as long as the younger child does not outgrow the older one.

—Aunt Becky

How We Relate

Circle Letters

A circle letter is started when ten or a dozen people living at different addresses make up a group, and the pack of letters goes round and round the circle, each member taking out his or her old letter and adding a new one every time the envelope comes to his or her mailbox. Some kinds of circle letters the Amish write:

1. Family letters—brothers and sisters, or cousins, living in different places.

2. Wheelchair writers—from these letters the housebound gathers courage and faith, for they tell of others [living] in the same way and overcoming the same temptations.

3. Teachers—from this experience of teachers writing to each other, the idea for an Amish teachers' magazine emerged. In the autumn of 1957, the *Blackboard Bulletin* was first published, consisting of articles by and for teachers.

4. Organic farmers.

5. Amish bakers.

6. Amish bishops.

7. Teenage girls.

8. Andy Mast Circle Letter—consisting of fourteen Amish with the same name, from Ohio to Ontario, aged twenty to eighty.

"Circles of friendship—that's what circle letters are."

—J. Stoll

The Greedy Heifer

One evening when I was helping my husband do the chores, I decided to feed the heifers so he would be done with his work sooner. First, I gave them a good helping of silage. On top of that, I heaped their feed supplement, which they liked even more. After I had fed them all and they were eating content-edly, I walked past them with another shovelful of silage to feed the dry cows. As I walked past, a young heifer tried to snatch a mouthful off the shovel, ignoring all the feed she had before herself.

"You silly, greedy heifer," I couldn't help but think. It was disgusting, really. She had all the feed in front of her that she could possibly eat, and yet she was trying to snatch away some of the other cows' silage.

Later, after thinking it over, I had to wonder how often we are in the eyes of God like that greedy heifer. We are blessed with plenty to eat, warm houses, good homes, family and friends, and all the material things we will ever be able to use and more. Yet we look about and lament when we see others who appear to have more than we do. Are we in the habit of counting our many blessings and appreciating all we have, or are we often wishing for and wanting what others have?

Sprinkling Cans

It was getting dry. The lettuce, celery, and cabbage seedlings we had transplanted needed to be watered for them to survive. Each morning I took the sprinkling can, filled it with water, and carried it to the garden. Each day I wished for rain, not only to be relieved of carrying water, but because the rest of the garden was suffering too. Then one morning the sky was overcast. At noon there were a few raindrops on the window. The clouds turned a shade darker. We waited hopefully.

Then the rain fell. Big drops fell to the ground and bounced like thousands of miniature marbles. I thought of our garden. It was being watered far beyond what I had been able to do in the past week or two. Not only was the whole garden being watered, but the yard, the pasture fields, the cornfields, the trees—acres and acres of crops for miles around would revive and yield better because of this rain. Gallons, no, tons of water were falling. My mind was too small to compare it with the two or three gallons I had been carrying each day. "Just think how small and meager my little sprinkling can is compared to a shower like this."

My friend thought a moment, then said, "But your sprinkling can kept the plants alive until this shower came. They would have died if you hadn't watered them."

Her statement, so simply stated, became a sermon that stuck in my mind long after we had both returned to our work. The more I thought about it, the more I realized that there were other "sprinkling cans" in our life.

The help we give our neighbors is small when we compare it with what God does for us. And yet the smallness of things we can do for each other does not give us the right to sit back and do nothing. Even though our "sprinkling cans" seem hopelessly small, our concerns and prayers and admonishments and good example must not cease as long as there is still hope. Oh, for more sprinkling cans—small vessels of love and peace, of goodwill and patience and hope!

Learning to Know Yourself

A few months ago we were in Fort Wayne, Indiana, to visit a couple of hospital patients. Then we stopped at a big clothing store. As we were walking around in there, I saw an elderly Amishman come walking toward me. "Now who is this old man?" I thought, and then I realized I was looking into a big glass mirror. I didn't know myself right away!

This started me to thinking that I should learn to know myself better, so this would not happen again. But then I had to think of how the Word of God is like a mirror, and how much more important it is that we learn to know ourselves in a spiritual sense, and see ourselves as we look in God's Word.

—Abe Lehman

The Better Plan

As a young married couple, my husband and I lived on a farm with Grandfather, who was a widower and the deacon of our church. One Sunday we discovered fresh car tracks beside our gas tank, close by the barn. We decided to keep an eye open during the nights and try to catch the thieves.

Sure enough, several nights later I awoke to hear a motor take off. I went to the window and saw the car drive away, the tank obviously filled with *our* gas. We were upset about it because we had a hard time making ends meet the way it was. We kept planning and thinking what we would do when they came again. We thought of draining the tank and putting in water. We even mentioned shooting into the air to frighten the thieves, or shooting into their tires to keep them from making a getaway.

Grandpa didn't like this idea. He said, "I will see if I can put a stop to it." He took a chain and fastened the hose to the spigot and locked it with a dial lock. He put a note on the tank that read, "If you need gas, come to the house, and we will give you some. That way you won't need to steal it." He signed his full name.

The next night at about two thirty, we again heard a car motor. We watched breathlessly. The thieves weren't there long. Then the motor started again, and they raced down the lane with their lights off until they reached the road. To this day they have not been back.

At first I thought the thieves got off much too easily. But as the years go by, I have often compared our attitude with

Grandpa's. I am sure that with our being Amish, they have more respect for our people than if we had used other methods. I also feel Grandpa's way as nearer to what Jesus would have done.

—Mrs. A. Y. M.

Heaven's Yardstick

The men of the community were building a new schoolhouse half a mile up the road. Since it was so near to home, William Yoder had told his wife, Mandy, not to pack his lunch; he would come home to eat and go back again.

As they began eating, Mandy said, "Well, how did it go at the school?"

William sighed. He dished out some potatoes for the two boys on either side of him, five-year-old Roy and three-year-old Elam. "It's going all right, I guess," he said. "It's just that I feel so dumb all the time. You know I'm no carpenter, and so often I don't know what to do or how to do it. I have to be asking all the time, and then it takes me longer than the others, especially longer than somebody like Ben Weaver and John Troyer. Either one of them can get four times as much done as I can."

After the meal was finished, William announced, "I sort of think I'll cultivate corn this afternoon."

"You mean you're not going back to the schoolhouse?" his wife asked.

"Oh, I don't think so. The little bit I get done won't make that much difference anyhow."

So that afternoon William Yoder didn't show up at the school frolic. Back in the house, Mandy felt sorry for her husband. Suddenly, she happened to think of something. She went to the calendar. Why, tomorrow was William's birthday. The least she could do was bake a cake for him. When the two boys, Roy and Elam, heard what she was doing and why, they wanted to make something for Daddy's birthday too.

"We want to color some pictures for Daddy," Elam said. "We haven't colored for a long time."

Mandy agreed that they could each color three pictures. "Happy birthday, Daddy!"

Their faces glowing, their eyes shining, Roy and Elam brought the pages they had colored. They had awakened earlier than usual this morning. As William paged through the pictures, Roy said, "You can tell which three are Elam's pictures. Do you know how?"

"How?"

"Well, look. He didn't stay inside the lines nearly as well as I did. His aren't as nice."

It was clear that he had tried hard, extraordinarily hard, but still Elam crossed over the line in many places.

"Oh, you shouldn't say they aren't as nice," William corrected. "They are real good for Elam. You see, he's not as old as you are. You both did the best you could, so to me Elam's pictures are the same."

To him, Elam's pictures did mean just as much as Roy's. Elam had probably worked harder than Roy had, even though a stranger would never guess it by looking at the finished product.

As William finished his chores that morning, a thought came to him that had never come to him before. Was it possible that the heavenly Father felt the same way about his children as an earthly father did? Was it possible that the heavenly Father also measured the worth of his children by their love and devotion, and not by the greatness of their deeds, or the extent of their accomplishments? Was it possible that the heavenly Father was just as pleased with the bungling and slow work

William Yoder did on the schoolhouse as he was with the expert craftsmanship and skill of Ben Weaver and John Troyer?

Quickly, William finished his chores. The corn could wait for another day. He hurried to the house to tell his wife of his change of plans. She would be surprised that he was going to the schoolhouse, but he knew she would approve. Somehow, [he was] going to do his part, however weak and awkward and imperfect, doing it with cheer and willingness. Wasn't that as good a way as any to celebrate his twenty-seventh birthday?

What William Yoder discovered on the day of his birthday, many more of us should perhaps also discover. The true measure of a man is not how many talents he possesses, but how well he uses those talents, whether they are great or small.

God does not measure us as much by our accomplishments as by our faithfulness in doing what we can. William learned a real lesson by the imperfect picture that his little boy Elam colored. The flaws of the picture did not destroy the beauty of the love and effort that colored it.

In the same way, some of us are like little Elam, awkward and clumsy and inexperienced. We try to stay inside the lines, but we do not always succeed. How comforting to know that the heavenly Father sees our intentions and willingness, and thus can find acceptable the work of our hands and hearts. We can rest in the knowledge that because of heaven's unusual yardstick, a person doing less may actually be doing more.

—E. Stoll

Free Rein

One day in late fall, snow fell and caught me unprepared for winter. Hoping to save a little time, I took a different way home, one with which I was not too familiar, yet I anticipated no problem. Old Dobbin obligingly trotted on, but I was not far until I began to have doubts that this road was leading me home. By now the only thing I was certain of was that I was not going where I wished to go.

A sudden inspiration came to me, and I urged my horse onward. I turned around and headed back the way I had come. Only this time I left it all to good old Dobbin. I knew I was too confused to decide for myself, and I believed that my horse wanted to get home every bit as much as I did. It was exactly the opposite of what seemed right to me, but I knew my hope was in trusting my horse and God, who had given him the homing instinct. We had not gone far before the faint outlines began to look familiar. My horse had found the way.

Is it not the same in our lives? We think we know, only to find ourselves on the wrong track. Our only way back is to turn around, let loose the reins, and trust Another to lead the way, even when it is not what we might choose for ourselves. We know he guides the way and knows our every need.

—*A Teacher*

Footprints

Last winter the ground was covered with a heavy snowfall. One day a man visited our farm to inquire about buying logs from our woods. He walked to the woods on a hill several fields away from the farm buildings. Later that evening I pointed out the footprints to the children. We admired the way they wound their way up the hill and disappeared into the woods.

Several weeks later it got warmer, and gradually the snow melted from the fields. One day I glanced toward the woods. There on the bare hillside were the footprints again, white and plain on the green and brown earth. The packed snow had not melted as fast as the rest, and we had a perfect set of footprints winding up the hill.

Each thought, action, and deed we do is a footprint. As they wind in and out through life, there are others about us who may look at them and notice the pattern they make.

Even after our life on earth is past, our footprints may remain. Perhaps the path we trod is one our children choose to follow. Or maybe it has influenced a neighbor who was looking for a guide to chart his course.

Where are our footprints leading?

—Beth Witmer

Postscript

I WANTED THE WRITERS who appear most frequently in this book to provide brief biographical sketches of themselves, to help readers get to know them a little as individuals. I also asked one of them to write a postscript. In response, I was respectfully informed, "We feel we will be getting enough publicity by having our names appear frequently in the book. There is no need to draw further attention to ourselves, or to in any way blow our own horns or that of Pathway."

In our modern world, where so many people seem to be promoting someone or something, often loudly and boastfully, this typical Amish attitude is refreshing. In a quiet manner, I was being told that it is not the *writers* who are significant; instead, if the ideas have value, it is the *words* that are important.

With so many negative stories and ideas bombarding us every day, I hope these writings will have some positive meaning for us. We can learn things from people who are different from ourselves. We can respect differences and even enjoy them. Sometimes in arguing our own point of view, we become closed to considering a different perspective. "Judge not, that you be not judged" (Matthew 7:1) is often quoted by the Amish. We can understand and even respect other ideas without necessarily agreeing with them or accepting them as our own. When we learn about a culture or way of thinking different from our own, we also can come to learn and understand *ourselves* better. We may like some of what we see; other aspects we may not. This is something we must learn to recognize, not deny.

Each culture is an expression of the growth of a society, religion, way of life, set of values. Each person in that society is an individual expression of the development, acceptance, or denial of those elements through personal experiences in that person's life and relationships.

In the Amish world, it is not the individual so much as the group that is important. Neither their world nor ours is perfect. Far from it. Yet the Amish believe we should focus not so much on visible things but rather on the coming world, God's kingdom. Thus these writers would not want to be praised for their writings or given any special attention.

Recognition should instead go to the faith and the God who has inspired them. Among the Amish, it is certainly appropriate to give credit to the writer, but to give the glory to God. May it be so.

—*Brad Igou*

THE COMPILER

Brad Igou has been president and co-owner of the Amish Experience in Lancaster County, Pennsylvania, and publisher of *Amish Country News*. Igou is past board chair of Discover Lancaster and recipient of its Lifetime Achievement Award. He also created the Amish Visit-in-Person Tour, which gives visitors the opportunity to personally meet and talk with the Amish where they live and work.

Stone Mantain RV front desk
770-413-5276